A Scrapbook of Christmas Firsts

A Scrapbook of Christmas Firsts

ISBN 978-0-89112-564-8

Printed in China

Scripture quotations, unless otherwise noted, are from The Holy Bible,
New International Version. Copyright 1984, International Bible Society.
Used by permission of Zondervan Publishers.

Design by Thinkpen Design, Inc. www.thinkpendesign.com

Leafwood Publishers
1648 Campus Court
Abilene, Texas 79601
1-877-816-4455
www.leafwoodpublishers.com

A Scrapbook of Christmas Firsts

Stories to Warm Your Heart and Tips to Simplify Your Holiday

Cathy Messecar
Terra Hangen Trish Berg
Karen Robbins
Leslie Wilson Brenda Nixon

Foreword

Who needs snow to have a perfect Christmas?

Discover true holiday joy in *A Scrapbook of Christmas Firsts.*

The Word Quilters compiled snippets of cheer and time-savers. The stories, recipes, family fun, and faith-filled hints will reward your quest for a meaningful, simpler holiday. A host of inspiration and ideas await you in these sections:

In Family Snapshot essays glimpse families who experienced Christmas firsts—a holiday campout, gifting a high school diploma, and a woman's loss of eyesight. Read heartwarming stories about a foster child in a new home, and find out what happened when Elvis attended the church Christmas party.

Gingerbread Genealogy brings you the history of many Christmas traditions, and **Vintage Poetry and Lyrics** allows a glance back into merry olde times. **Peppermints for Little Ones** suggests ways to engage children in sharing and giving to others. **Stocking Stuffer Tradition** offers help for connecting family members.

In a Gift for You, we offer ways to create holiday fun and simplify. Got a sweet tooth and not much time? Plunge your hand into our **Cookie Canister** and pull out one of our easy, sweet recipes. For Christmas gardening and infusing the fresh-cut scent of pines into your home, look for **Evergreen Thumb** tips.

A Few of Our Favorite Things lists Christmas books, outdoor activities, and more. In **Trivia Treasures**, discover Christmas facts about the first state to declare Christmas a legal holiday, about honoring the fallen at Arlington National Cemetery, and about the North Pole Marathon.

Under **Bethlehem Star**, read twelve Scriptures about Jesus and at **Morning Star Light**, twelve sayings uttered by Jesus. In **Word Quilters' Wisdom** we present a simple thought to tuck away for a day, a season, or a lifetime.

When you need fresh ideas, a stress-free Christmas, a return to the basics, who can you turn to? The Word Quilters.

We're dedicated to helping you uncomplicate Christmas and usher in the goodwill that celebrates a Savior and family.

Merry Christmas to all!

Firstborn Son

In those days Caesar Augustus issued a decree that a census should be taken of the entire Roman world. (This was the first census that took place while Quirinius was governor of Syria.) And everyone went to his own town to register.

So Joseph also went up from the town of Nazareth in Galilee to Judea, to Bethlehem the town of David, because he belonged to the house and line of David. He went there to register with Mary, who was pledged to be married to him and was expecting a child. While they were there, the time came for the baby to be born, and she gave birth to her firstborn, a son. She wrapped him in cloths and placed him in a manger, because there was no room for them in the inn.

And there were shepherds living out in the fields nearby, keeping watch over their flocks at night. An angel of the Lord appeared to them, and the glory of the Lord shone around them, and they were terrified. But the angel said to them, "Do not be afraid. I bring you good news of great joy that will be for all the people. Today in the town of David a Savior has been born to you; he is Christ the Lord. This will be a sign to you: You will find a baby wrapped in cloths and lying in a manger."

Suddenly a great company of heavenly host appeared with the angel, praising God and saying,

"Glory to God in the highest,
  and on earth peace to men on
  whom his favor rests."

When the angels had left them and gone into heaven, the shepherds said to one another, "Let's go to Bethlehem and see this thing that has happened, which the Lord has told us about."

So they hurried off and found Mary and Joseph, and the baby, who was lying in the manger. When they had seen him, they spread the word concerning what had been told them about this child, and all who heard it were amazed at what the shepherds said to them. But Mary treasured up all these things and pondered them in her heart. The shepherds returned, glorifying and praising God for all the things they had heard and seen, which were just as they had been told.

LUKE 2:1-20

Table of Contents

CHAPTER ONE

Once Upon a Christmas

For nothing is impossible with God. LUKE 1:37

AN INFERTILE COUPLE CONCEIVES, A SOLDIER RETURNS FROM A WAR ZONE,

A DISEASE GOES INTO REMISSION, ENEMIES SHAKE HANDS—DREAMS ARE

MADE OF SUCH THINGS. PLACE YOUR DREAMS INTO GOD'S HANDS.

FAMILY SNAPSHOT

Home for Christmas

BY KAREN E. HOOD

Memory lane—a permanent street in my mind—runs through my childhood. One of my favorite places to stop is the first Christmas with my parents. The wonder of Christmas came alive that year. For ten months I had lived with my new parents.

Eight years old, I'd been assigned to foster parents before, in fact several times. As so often with children in foster care, I moved from home to home. But this time it was different. This family planned to keep me, to adopt me.

We lived on a dairy farm where the pastures hugged the foothills, graced with fir, pine, and laurel trees. I took to tromping in those woods on various trails and when December arrived, I joined my parents on a trek into the forest to cut a Christmas tree. This search was a new adventure for me—such excitement this exploration for that perfect tree!

In the days that followed, Dad, Mom, and I brought nature into the house: boughs of evergreen, pine cones, and holly. Bright red berries decorated the mantel, and the hand-picked tree stood in a corner, popcorn and cranberry strands looped over its branches. A flurry of other activities filled our days: baking, shopping for gifts, and wrapping presents.

In our home, a nativity reminded me that the true spirit of Christmas was in the birth of Christ. And, near the end of December, I participated in our church program and children's choir.

On Christmas Eve, my new extended family gathered. Carols played, and we settled in for our evening meal, a deliberately light fare since we'd feast the next day. That night we ate clam chowder, crackers and cheese, and sampled the goodies baked in previous days.

After the meal, we moved into the living room around the tree. I learned that my family opened a few gifts on Christmas eve and then on Christmas morning opened Santa's gifts. The anticipation of uncovering the treasures hidden in colorful boxes left me wide eyed and eager.

For a little girl who had arrived in this home with barely the clothes on her back, I felt rich beyond my imagination. I opened my first gift. Handmade pajamas from my mother! Most of the gifts I received that evening were things I so desperately needed.

Soon it was time to scamper up to bed with the promise of Santa arriving before morning. I put on my new pajamas and snuggled into the covers, too excited to fall right to sleep. Even as a child I was never a morning person, but that first Christmas in my new home I awoke early.

I sneaked down the stairs to see if Santa had found my new location. To my delight he had! Mom and Dad were waiting for me. My stocking overflowed with nuts, a candy cane, and an orange. In front of the fireplace sat a rocking chair and a doll—for me.

I couldn't wait to wrap my arms around her and hold something of my very own. I sat in my new chair and picked up the doll. That's when I knew God had given me an even greater gift than the doll. He gave me the gift of parents and a home for Christmas.

I belonged.

BETHLEHEM STAR

For to us a child is born, to us a son is given,
and the government will be on his shoulders.
And he will be called Wonderful Counselor,
Mighty God, Everlasting Father, Prince of Peace.

—ISAIAH 9:6

GINGERBREAD GENEALOGY

Candy Canes ~ Terra Hangen

Does every family in America hang candy canes on their Christmas tree? In my family candy canes are considered essential ornaments. If someone forgets to buy them, a candy cane aficionado will point out that our tree, with its limbs sagging from a myriad of ornaments, looks downright naked. This causes an emergency run to the local candy cane emporium.

The king of canes in the United States is the red and white variety, but the first candy sticks were pure white and straight in shape. These white confections, created 350 years ago, were first bent into the shape of a cane or shepherd's staff in 1670 by the frustrated choirmaster at the Cologne Cathedral in Germany.

Each year unruly children disrupted the music during the very long Nativity services, until the choirmaster had the brilliant idea to bend the canes to look like a shepherd's staff, and give them to the children during Nativity services. This gambit worked so well that candy canes were soon doled out at Christmas church services throughout Europe.

The candy cane first appeared in America in 1847. A German immigrant, August Imgard, decorated his tree in Wooster, Ohio, with them. The first red and white striped canes were introduced early in the twentieth century. Soon after, candy makers added peppermint and wintergreen flavors.

Remember to buy extra canes for guests, stocking stuffers, and those tree trimmers who can't resist sampling while they work.

VINTAGE LYRICS

O morning stars, together
Proclaim the holy birth!
And praises sing to God the King,
And peace to men on earth.
For Christ is born of Mary,
And gathered all above,
While mortals sleep, the angels keep
Their watch of wondering love.

FROM "O LITTLE TOWN OF BETHLEHEM"
BY PHILLIPS BROOKS (1835-1893)

STOCKING STUFFER TRADITIONS

LESLIE WILSON

On the Christmas table, place an unlit candle at each person's place.
During the meal, the host lights the candle of the person seated
to his left, offering encouragement or telling something
that he loves about that person. Continue
around the table.

A FEW OF OUR FAVORITE THINGS
Christmas Charities

BRENDA, KAREN, LESLIE

Samaritan's Purse, Operation Christmas Child: http://www.samaritanspurse.org/

Leslie: "I loved helping my kids shop for items for Operation Christmas Child each year for our MOPS (Mothers of Preschoolers). They buy candy, small gifts, and household items for a child living in an underprivileged area of the world."

CATHY

Oxfam America: www.oxfamamericaunwrapped.com

Through donations, give gifts that benefit others year-round: a donkey, goat, sheep, camel, or a dozen chickens, or crop-gifts such as seeds or trees. Give in someone's name and Oxfam will send them an attractive card with a similar photo of the gift through snail mail or e-mail.

TRISH

Salvation Army Adopt-a-Family: http://www.salvationarmyusa.org

We adopt a family, get their Christmas wish list, and Mike and I take our kids to shop for the family. We then wrap and deliver their presents—a great way for kids to help others.

TERRA

Marine Corps Toys for Tots: www.toysfortots.org

In all 50 states, donate unwrapped new toys.

TRIVIA TREASURES

I n mid-December, Arlington National Cemetery graves receive five thousand fresh green Christmas wreaths with red bows. Worcester Wreath Company of Maine started the tradition. Owner Morrill Worcester had a dream of doing something for those who gave their lives for this nation. "We couldn't do anything in this country if it wasn't for the people who gave their lives to protect us."

The wreaths are laid out in about one hour with different branches of the military and civilians helping. Four are placed at the Tomb of the Unknown Soldier. Tech. Sgt. Lisa Rodier, who has helped at least four years, describes the event as "very emotional." She wishes everyone could experience honoring our fallen.

Wreaths of America accepts donations to place garlands at National Cemeteries across our nation: www.wreaths-across-america.org

PEPPERMINTS FOR LITTLE ONES

TRISH BERG

Early in December, place a $10 roll of quarters in your car.
Allow children to give a quarter each time you walk
near a Salvation Army kettle.

A GIFT FOR YOU

Balloon Bouquet ~ LESLIE WILSON

Insert "work chores" and "fun chores" into red and green balloons. Blow up balloons, attach long curly ribbons, and tape them near the Christmas dinner table. After the meal, each person pulls a ribbon, bursts the balloon, reads the note, and does what it says.

Examples of chores:

- "Help clear the table."
- "Serve the dessert."
- "Hug the person on your left."
- "Take extra chairs back to the kitchen."
- "Tell about your best Christmas."
- "Relax, put your feet up, and take a nap."
  Put an identifying mark on this one and save it for yourself.

Orange Sour Cream Cookies ~ CATHY MESSECAR

2 1/2 cups flour	2 eggs	Frosting (prepare before baking cookies)
1 tsp. soda	1 tsp. vanilla	1 1/2 Tbs. soft butter
1/2 tsp. salt	1 tsp. grated orange rind	1 1/2 Tbs. grated orange rind
1/2 cup butter	1 cup sour cream	3 Tbs. orange juice
1 1/2 cups brown sugar		3 cups confectioner's sugar

Sift dry ingredients, cream butter and sugar, add eggs, vanilla, orange rind, and sour cream. Stir in dry ingredients, add nuts. Drop by tsp. onto greased cookie sheets. Bake at 350°, 10-12 minutes. Top each warm cookie with 1/2 tsp. frosting. Yield: 4 dozen

EVERGREEN THUMB

Myrrh ~ TERRA HANGEN

To honor the Christ Child, the wise men traveled long miles on camels to give him the greatest gifts their civilization knew: gold, frankincense, and myrrh. Try this biblical plant in your garden.

A few nurseries sell seedlings of this shrubby tree during Advent season, but these plants may be difficult to find. A substitute, the Torote or Elephant Tree (Bursera microphylla) is the New World's closest relative to myrrh, and like its cousin exudes a resin that when dry can be burned as fragrant incense.

Horizon Herbs in Oregon sells 10 Torote seeds for about $10. www.horizonherbs.com

The Light in My Heart

BY JAN ECKLES

"**O** Lord. I was doing so well," I muttered, fighting back the tears. I stepped into my bedroom and the flood of tears poured out. I didn't want my three-, five-, and seven-year-old sons to watch me cry. Not at Christmas time. Not while they opened their presents with shouts of glee and expressions of surprise.

My loss of sight had thrust me into a new mode of operation. As the season began, I'd kept my composure. I faced my loss of sight with resignation, perhaps even with a bit of courage. Solo Christmas shopping was an adventure I missed, but my husband's loving assistance helped ease the unwanted adjustment.

I remember walking the store aisles with him. I'd give him suggestions, or as he found possibilities, he sought my input. "Honey, what do you think about this Nintendo game for Jason?"

Without thinking, I gave the usual response, "Let me see." But as soon as those words slipped from my lips, the reality of my blindness gripped my heart—there was nothing to see.

Gone were the days when I'd hopped in the car with list in hand, hit the department store sales, and come home with surprises for everyone in the family. I forced myself to dismiss thoughts of the past and focus on the shopping task at hand.

Although my loss of independence gnawed at me, I was determined to do—by myself—the decorating of the house for Christmas, no matter how long it took. I lined all the boxes holding the decorations against the wall out of my walking path.

"Are you sure I can't help you?" my husband asked.

"Thanks. But you already helped me enough with wrapping the presents. I'll be okay." My fingers told me the shape of each item in the boxes, and immediately its image popped into my mind. Next, with careful steps to avoid tripping over obstacles on the floor or bumping into the furniture, I found the perfect spot for each decoration.

After placement of the last item, I said to myself, "There! I finally did it."

Images of a red and green winter land danced in my head. I learned to rely on memories, and fought back the painful nostalgia of my days with sight. That first Christmas season without my sight, I said "Thank you, Lord" many times over, truly grateful that He sustained me moment after moment.

Christmas morning came and three pairs of little feet bounced around our bed.

"I want to open presents!" Joe cried out.

"Me too!" echoed Jason and Jeff.

I fumbled to find my robe, slipped it on, and followed their cheerful voices. They made my heart smile. As we entered our family room, pine scent filled the air and little boy sounds bounced around the room and filled my heart.

"Okay, we have to do this in order," I said. "Daddy will give one to each of you and you open it when we tell you."

"Me first!" shouted our youngest. "Wow! This is cool!" I glanced in his direction, but a veil of gray covered my view. Everything in me longed to see the expression of his little face. What did he open? What made him so excited?

I blinked back tears, chided myself—why can't you just enjoy what you hear? The more "Ohs" and "Ahs" that reached my ears, the more I became overwhelmed with desire to see even a glimpse. "I'll be right back," I said and rose from the couch with outstretched arms to feel my way down the wall. I headed to my bedroom.

My eyes burned as I fought the tears. Slumped down on the bed, I wondered: "Lord, why is this affecting me so. Please help me to understand. Show me how to cope . . . I don't know how."

In the middle of my sobs, I heard my husband come in. I felt his arms encircle me. "What can I do for you, honey?"

"I'm okay." I brushed my tears with the back of my hand.

"Mommy, Daddy, can we open some more?" Joe called out.

"I'll be there in a moment," I called back. I whispered to my husband, "I don't want to ruin things." I yanked a tissue from the box on our dresser and tried to swallow my pain, but instead a deep sigh escaped.

"This is the best present of all!" one of my sons shouted. His words struck me like a sudden cold draft. Jolted, the darkness lifted from my heart. I'd been dwelling on what I couldn't see, and I'd missed God's present to me, the best one of all—my family.

In my desperation to see my surroundings, I'd failed to gaze into the very thing that brightened my new-formed world. I rejoined my sons Joe, Jason, and Jeff in the family room and, although I couldn't see their faces, I listened more closely to their giggles, shouts of joy, and innocent questions that revealed what was in their young hearts.

On this first Christmas without my sight, God replaced my physical sight with "insight," and like the star atop the Christmas tree, profound gratitude shone within my soul.

MORNING STAR LIGHT

If I make you light-bearers, you don't think
I'm going to hide you under a bucket, do you?
I'm putting you on a light stand.
Now that I've put you there on a hilltop,
on a light stand—shine!

MATTHEW 5:15, THE MESSAGE

WORD QUILTERS' WISDOM

Dream big and wait—
for nothing is impossible with God.

CHAPTER TWO

Lost and Found

She will give birth to a son, and you are to give him the name Jesus, because he will save his people from their sins. MATTHEW 1:21

IN CAROLS, CARDS, AND MEDIA, CHRISTMAS LANGUAGE SPEAKS
OF GOOD WILL, PEACE, AND FAMILY. DURING THIS SEASON OF CHEER,
CHOOSE TO NURTURE RELATIONSHIPS AND RECLAIM LOST CONTACTS.

FAMILY SNAPSHOT

Christmas Dinner at Waffle House

BY CHARLOTTE HOLT

"Y ou want to travel on Christmas Day? You want to go now?" I couldn't believe my husband, Charles, wanted to make an unplanned trip to Arlington, Texas. I looked at him dumbfounded and discovered he was serious.

"Why not? We've opened our gifts, and we really don't have anything else to do," he reasoned.

I glanced at my son, Louis. "What do you think? Would you like to go to Arlington?"

"It's okay with me. I'm with you guys. I'm just glad to spend Christmas with you."

I couldn't say anything for a few moments because of the lump in my throat. This year, my prodigal son had changed his life and come home for Christmas vacation with a good attitude and drug free. He now attended college and worked on a certification in graphic design, but many years of his life had been spent in the drug culture—using, buying, and selling drugs. During that time, my heart broke again and again. Most of the time, I didn't know his whereabouts or if he was alive or dead. On occasion, he called from jails or prison. I never knew what to expect. At one point, I didn't hear from him for three years. When I didn't know where he was, I agonized. The pain often grew deeper when I did—for I knew his lifestyle.

What a welcome change when he decided to straighten out his life and go to school. It was wonderful to have him home for the holidays—the first in many years.

The three of us discussed the matter and decided to hit the road for Arlington, Texas, for a couple of days to visit with Charles's sister and family.

"We can't make it for Christmas dinner, you know. They eat at noon. It's already after ten." I reminded them of the five-hour drive.

"That's okay." Charles said, "We can stop and eat along the way."

I envisioned stopping at Sam's, one of my favorite restaurants, midway on the trip. Then I remembered the holiday. "Do you think Sam's will be open?"

"If not, we can find something," Charles said.

We each went to pack. My husband loves doing something different and often on the spur of the moment. I like to plan ahead, but give in to his whims more often than not. Besides, I expected we would enjoy the trip. Charles and God have a way of making things turn out good.

We loaded the car with Christmas gifts and took off down the road. By the time we reached halfway on our trip, stomachs growled. We searched for a restaurant. Sam's wasn't open. We passed several eating places but the same sign hung in each storefront—Closed.

Finally, in the middle of nowhere, a Waffle House loomed. Relieved, we noticed cars surrounded the restaurant. "I can't believe we will eat lunch on Christmas Day at a Waffle House," I said. "This will be a first for me."

"I've eaten many holiday meals there. It's about the only thing open on those days," Louis said. "Sometimes a stranger would buy my lunch."

Another lump formed in my throat and tears stung my eyes. How many lonely Christmases had my son spent on the road eating alone or with some drug-addicted friend?

My mood changed. This was my first Christmas to eat at a Waffle House, but I was happy to dine anywhere with my son. I felt thankful for the food, but even more grateful to be together with my returned prodigal.

When Charles offered the blessing over our food, I thanked God in my heart for this first, and I prayed for the beginning of many more great adventurous holidays spent with my son.

BETHELEHEM STAR

He won't brush aside the bruised and the hurt
and he won't disregard the small and insignificant,
but he'll steadily and firmly set things right.

ISAIAH 42:3, THE MESSAGE

GINGERBREAD GENEALOGY

Christmas Day ~ Leslie Wilson

During the first century, only the date of death was recorded into family histories, so we cannot know Jesus' exact birth date. Also, because Christ is divine, the early church thought recognizing his birth reduced Jesus to the level of an earthly king.

Scripture indicates the baby Jesus most likely arrived in the spring, not winter. "And there were shepherds living out in the fields nearby, keeping watch over their flocks at night" (Luke 2:8 niv). Sheep were only out of corrals during lambing time, in the spring and early summer.

The Roman Catholic Church established a celebration on December 25th to overshadow that of a rival pagan ritual that threatened the existence of Christianity, according to Alan Varasdi in *Myth Information.* In the early fourth century, pagan Romans—who comprised the majority at the time—celebrated *Natalis Solis Invincti* or "Birthday of the Invincible Sun God," Mithras.

Christians desired an alternative to the pagan rituals—one that would celebrate Jesus' birth. December 25th was chosen to set up the Nativity and celebrate Christ's Mass. A tradition began. The birthday assigned to Jesus is now celebrated over the entire world.

VINTAGE POETRY

I heard the bells on Christmas Day
Their old, familiar carols play,
And wild and sweet
The words repeat
Of peace on earth, good-will to men!

FROM "CHRISTMAS BELLS" BY
HENRY WADSWORTH LONGFELLOW

STOCKING STUFFER TRADITIONS

Nativity ~ LESLIE WILSON

Set out an unbreakable nativity set and allow young children to play with it. Adults and older children can take turns reading the Christmas story from Luke 2 while younger ones add the characters to the scene.

A FEW OF OUR FAVORITE THINGS

Christmas Books

BRENDA

<u>God Rest Ye Grumpy Scroogeymen</u>, by Laura Jensen Walker and Michael K. Walker

A nonfiction book about restoring fun at Christmastime

CATHY

<u>A Christmas Train</u>, a novel by David Baldacci

A journalist, banned from the airlines, rides a train and finds Christmas warmth

KAREN

<u>Skipping Christmas</u>, a novel by John Grisham

Hilarity on the home front when the Kranks decide to skip Christmas

LESLIE

<u>The Christmas Box</u>, by Richard Paul Evans

A touching tale of a widow and a family who moves into her home

TERRA

<u>A Cup of Christmas Tea</u>, by Tom Hegg and Warren Hanson

Rhyming verse about a visit to an elderly aunt's home

TRISH

<u>The Old Fashioned Country Christmas</u>, by Gooseberry Patch

A keepsake of recipes, traditions, decorating ideas, and childhood memories

TRIVIA TREASURES

In 1836, the state of Alabama first declared Christmas a holiday. In 1856, President Franklin Pierce decorated the first White House Christmas tree, and in 1907, Oklahoma became the last state to sanction Christmas as a legal holiday.

PEPPERMINTS FOR LITTLE ONES

Knotty Countdown ~ Leslie Wilson

Tie knots in a short rope, one for each day
remaining until Christmas, and hang it on your
child's doorknob. Each night, untie one knot.

Hone the Holidays ~ CATHY MESSECAR

Perhaps it's time to pare Christmas traditions. Do you really need to buy suet and concoct Great Aunt Thelma's plum pudding—dark pudding prone to lurk in the fridge until June?

List the customs your family celebrates: special recipes, community events, holiday movies, stockings by the fireplace, outdoor decorations, etc. Early in December, go over this list with family members. What traditions have lost their meaning? Is someone a stickler for the plum pudding? Negotiate which traditions to keep and which to drop. Enlist the help of family to carry out their newly sanctioned holiday plans.

COOKIE CANISTER

Nutmeg Logs ~ TRISH BERG

"This cookie recipe was passed from my mother-in-law, Mary Ann, to me, and has become one of our family favorites."

1 cup soft butter	1 egg	*Icing*	2 cups sifted confectioner's sugar
2 tsp. vanilla	3 cups sifted flour	$1/3$ cup butter	2 Tbs. milk.
2 tsp. rum flavoring	2 tsp. nutmeg	1 tsp. vanilla	Beat until smooth and creamy
$3/4$ cup sugar	$1/4$ tsp. salt	2 tsp. rum flavoring	

Cream butter with flavorings. Gradually beat in sugar. Blend in egg. Sift flour, 1 tsp. nutmeg, and salt. Add to butter mixture. Mix well. Shape dough on sugared cutting board into log shaped rolls about $1/2$ inch in diameter. Cut into 3-inch lengths and place on buttered cookie sheets. Bake at 350° 12 to 15 minutes. Cool on rack. After icing, sprinkle nutmeg on log. Yield: 4 dozen

EVERGREEN THUMB

Re-blooming Poinsettias ~ TERRA HANGEN

Red, white, pink, and peach poinsettias grace homes at Christmas. Instead of throwing out your poinsettia after the holidays, help it re-bloom next Christmas.

In February or early March, cut the plant back to 4 inches tall. Keep it in a sunny window, water when dry, and in summer move the poinsettia outside. In the fall, bring it inside before the night temperature is below 60 degrees.

Beginning October 1, poinsettias need complete darkness from 5 p.m. to 8 a.m., achieved by placing in a dark closet. Keep the poinsettia in a closet at night, but set it in a sunny window in daytime. Provide temperatures from 55 to 70 degrees, water when dry, and fertilize once a month.

On December 15, when the leaves or bracts become colorful and almost fully formed, the darkness treatment is complete. Stop applying fertilizer. Find a sunny spot for it in your house, water when dry, and show off your re-bloomed poinsettia gem.

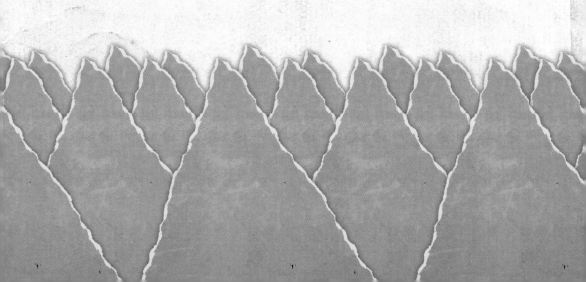

The Jesse Tree

BY JAN TICKNER

With a steamy cup of cider in hand, I sat eyeing the collective handiwork of now-grown family members. Our entire house, adorned with greenery, bows, and treasures, centered round the handsome, artificial tree bedecked with delicate baubles and bangles. Standing tall, the tree maintained its watch over mounds of beautifully wrapped packages. Limbs dripped with carefully placed silver icicles, strings of multi-colored lights, and garlands of golden beadery.

Impressive?

Perhaps. But an intense feeling of dissatisfaction dimmed my usual joy. It's what Mama used to call "a sinking spell." All the storybook symbols of this Advent season suddenly lost their luster. I felt it was time to take a "first" step toward radical, outward changes in our lives, reflecting glorious, inward changes.

That's the day we assembled a Jesse Tree.

A Jesse Tree?

The concept, described in one of our children's old Sunday school take-home booklets, came from Isaiah's prophecy: "And there shall come forth a Shoot out of the stock of Jesse, David's father, and a Branch out of his roots shall grow and bear fruit" (11:1 Amplified).

My husband Russ joined me in assembling a Jesse tree. With each crude, but lovingly fashioned ornament, the birth and ancestry of our Lord Jesus came to life. We fashioned such items as a carved apple missing two bites, representing Adam and Eve and the promise of a redeemer.

Together, we handily constructed small wooden pieces such as Noah's ark and Jacob's ladder. I added a tiny, many-colored coat for Joseph, a sheaf of wheat for Ruth, a small lamb for Abraham and Isaac, and a star for Esther. Finally, from a small piece of wood, Russ carved a rough-hewn cross to place atop the miniature tree. Biblical history—His-Story would be reflected in its branches.

On the small evergreen, we draped multi-strands of dainty white lights along with chains of miniature golden stars. We hung the handmade ornaments, and the little tree took its rightful place in the family room.

But the change did not stop there. A week later my husband's additional handiwork—a straw-filled, life-sized, wooden slatted manger—replaced the long-hallowed, traditional Christmas tree. In an attempt to make it a scene instead of display, I placed a three-legged milking stool, a wooly-white lamb, and even a basket of corn next to the crib.

We knew the removal of the traditional tree would be the supreme test with family and friends. How would they react seeing their life-time staid observance gone? Would any be disappointed or offended?

First, however, before the disclosure, there was still the quest for a "baby" to place in the manger. Daily, I trudged in and out of stores, digging through shelves stacked high with dollies of every size and shape.

Pouty faces, wooly hair, and blank expressions greeted me, dressed in every conceivable style from velveteen Fauntleroy suits, to sports uniforms, and even a few rugged caveman skins. Time grew short, but I didn't give up. Would this driving desire to give witness to our Lord fail?

Finally, I found the right doll. Still uneasy, however, I needed confirmation. It came when family and friends gathered for dinner. My grandson Micah immediately spied the manger scene. I held my breath. Awestruck, he exclaimed, "Oh, it's baby Jesus!"

His reaction stirred the entire group and caused me to remember walking into the small select doll shop where I sensed I would find the baby for the manger to make our very first Christmas with the Jesse tree and the stable scene complete.

To the owner, I had boldly announced, "I'm looking for Baby Jesus."

She had smiled and nodded, as if to say, "Isn't everybody?"

MORNING STAR LIGHT

Come, follow me.

MATTHEW 4:19

WORD QUILTERS' WISDOM

The one who re-scripts lives and erases
past blunders—his Father named him Jesus.

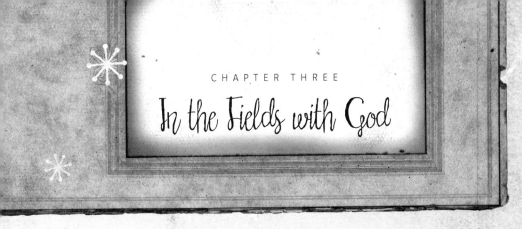

CHAPTER THREE

In the Fields with God

*And there were shepherds living out in the fields
nearby, keeping watch over their flocks at night.* LUKE 2:8

DURING THE HOLIDAYS, PLASTIC AND MANMADE GREENERY

ABOUND. FOR REAL CHRISTMAS MAGIC, GO OUTDOORS.

FAMILY SNAPSHOT

First Christmas Campout

BY TERRA HANGEN

For some glorious reason, my mom and dad celebrated Christmas one year by taking my sister, Sky, and me and our little Chihuahua, Chili Rey King of Martini, camping in the wild Florida Everglades. Our school excused us a few extra days before Christmas vacation, thrilling us. Our camping gear strapped to the top of the old green Plymouth station wagon, shark-like tail fins rising above the back fenders, we began the drive from Wisconsin to Florida.

We practiced true camping. According to my family's definition, camping is not sleeping in a vehicle, a.k.a. a metal box, a.k.a. a camper van, with electricity and the conveniences of home. True camping for our family of four, meant pitching a tent. Contented, we snuggled into sleeping bags in our no-frills green canvas tent, boasting a screened-in porch. Our sleeping bags were on cots. A touch of luxury, yes, but they would keep the Everglades snakes away from us.

This was a BIG adventure for girls who usually spent each Christmas in a warm home with a gigantic Christmas tree decorated with countless ornaments, dreaming of sugar plums and gifts to come, and church on Christmas day.

On our drive south, we spent one night in a motel and swam in an outdoor heated pool, and then ran shivering to our room. As we neared the Everglades, we saw a man alongside the road holding up an eight-foot dead rattlesnake. We loved the Everglades with its mysterious evasive panthers, menacing alligators, and extravagantly plumed herons and egrets. We strolled along raised wooden walkways deep into the swamps. For 8- and 13-year-old girls, it seemed we had ventured into wild territory. At our campsite we hand fed peanuts to pet-like chipmunks and walked in the starlit night to the park rangers' campfire talks.

We continued our drive even farther south to the Florida Keys. On Sanibel Island beaches we gathered seashells and were stunned to find roads and driveways made from crushed white shells. Some driveway-shells appeared perfectly collectible, and a jovial motel owner encouraged us to scoop up what we wanted.

Colorful Macaw parrots in riotous yellows, reds, blues, and greens sat on our shoulders in Parrot Jungle. We toured Viscaya Mansion, built ocean side with its own cement island, shaped like a sailing ship.

We learned how anhingas earned their creepy nickname "snakebirds." As the anhinga swims below the surface of the swamp waters, its long, thin black neck and head remain above the water, resembling a black snake.

Our family bought a small Christmas tree and decorated it with items we found around camp, including can lids and berries. Christmas Eve ushered unusual cold into the Everglades. The next morning, we thrilled to find a layer of ice in a water bucket left outside the tent.

Sky and I don't remember what material gifts were under the tiny tree, but the gift that lasts is the memory of our first and only Christmas campout with the family we loved most in the entire universe.

BETHLEHEM STAR

Watch for this: A girl who is presently a virgin will get pregnant. She'll bear a son and name him Immanuel (God-With-Us).

ISAIAH 7:14, THE MESSAGE

GINGERBREAD GENEALOGY

Christmas Tree Spider ~ TERRA HANGEN

A humble spider watched in awe as a family decorated a Christmas tree. The little spider yearned to contribute to the beauty of the tree, sparkling with colors. When the family went to bed on Christmas Eve, the spider slowly climbed the tree, examining each ornament.

As he climbed from branch to branch, ornament to ornament, the tiny spider left a web behind him, tracing his journey all over the tree. When Santa Claus arrived, so legend says, he turned the webs into silver and gold that gleamed with a holy light.

On Christmas morning, the tree covered in brilliant webs entranced the family.

The story of the small spider led to the tradition of hanging spider ornaments on Christmas trees. All of God's creatures add to the beauty of holiday trees—reindeer, golden fish, rare tigers, parrots, horses, dogs, cats, and flying pigs find homes on fresh and artificial trees. Why not the spider?

The story of the Christmas spider, like many ornament tales, originated long ago in Germany. Our Christmas tree boasts two lovely spider ornaments, both gifts from Wisconsin and Indiana relatives, where German traditions are strong. The ornaments grace our tree in honor of the little spider who contributed to the beauty of Christmas.

VINTAGE LYRICS

Come, Thou Bright and Morning Star,
Light of light, without beginning!
Shine upon us from afar
That we may be kept from sinning.
Drive away by Thy clear light
Our dark night.

Let Thy grace, like morning dew
Falling soft on barren places,
Comfort, quicken, and renew
Our dry souls and dying graces;
Bless Thy flock from Thy rich store
Evermore.

COME, THOU BRIGHT AND MORNING STAR
AN EXCERPT, BY CHRISTIAN K. VON ROSENROTH 1636-1689
TRANSLATED BY RICHARD MASSIE, 1800-1887

STOCKING STUFFER TRADITIONS

Creature Brunch ~ LESLIE WILSON

Decorate an outdoor tree with food ornaments: garlands
of cranberries and popcorn, pinecones painted
with peanut butter and rolled in birdseed.

A FEW OF OUR FAVORITE THINGS

Outdoor Christmas Celebrations

BRENDA ~ **Precious Moments Chapel, Carthage, Missouri**

http://www.preciousmoments.com/park/attractions

CATHY ~ **Dickens on the Strand, Galveston, Texas, annual, first weekend in December**

http://www.dickensonthestrand.org

KAREN ~ **Grand Illumination at Williamsburg, Williamsburg, Virginia**

http://www.history.org/christmas/

TERRA ~ **Christmas in The Park, San Jose, California**

www.christmasinthepark.com

Four hundred trees decorated by nonprofit groups, animated displays: Reindeer Barn, Swiss Clock Maker, Ornament Mine, and outdoor ice skating among palm trees. Free, 40,000 attend each year over the course of five weeks

TRISH ~ **The Polar Express Train Ride**

http://www.polarexpressride.com/schedules.html

Based on the great book, <u>Polar Express</u>, many states have their own version of this train ride. They serve cookies and hot cocoa, and ticket holders wear snuggly warm pajamas.

(F)or decades, the Province of Nova Scotia has presented a Christmas tree to the city of Boston in gratitude for relief supplies. In 1917, after a collision of ships in the Halifax, Nova Scotia harbor, many buildings lining the harbor collapsed, killing thousands. The citizens of Boston, the first to reach the site, supplied aid to their neighbors.

Easy Coconut Macaroons ~ CATHY MESSECAR

3 egg whites	$1/8$ tsp. salt
1 cup sugar	$1/2$ tsp. almond flavoring
2 Tbs. flour	$1^1/_2$ cups shredded sweetened coconut

Combine egg whites and sugar. Stir until sugar is dissolved. Mix in remaining ingredients. Line baking pan with greased brown paper or baking parchment. Drop by teaspoonfuls onto paper. Optional: press almonds or candied cherries into top of macaroons before baking. Bake at 350° for about 20 minutes. Yield: 2 dozen.

A GIFT FOR YOU

Budgeting for Next Christmas ~ CATHY MESSECAR

December 15th through January, many overstocked items such as Christmas cards, décor, and disposable tableware go on sale. Stock up for the next year, at prices discounted as much as 50 percent off or more. Store the sale items with Christmas decorations you display earliest, so the bargain-finds are not forgotten.

PEPPERMINTS FOR LITTLE ONES

A White Christmas ~ Karen Robbins

Items needed:

disposable plastic tray with foam base (meat tray—no metal)

pine cones	plastic animals	twigs	6 Tbs. bluing
little houses, cars	1 Tbs. household ammonia	6 Tbs. salt	6 Tbs. water

Create a landscape on the tray by gluing the pine cones, twigs, etc., firmly in place. Mix together salt, bluing, water, and ammonia. Spritz water on the landscape to make it moist and then pour the mixture over all the items in your landscape. In a few hours, "snowflakes" will begin to form. These will grow for a few days. They are fragile so place your tray where it can be seen but not touched by little hands.

EVERGREEN THUMB

Mistletoe ~ TERRA HANGEN

Kissing under the mistletoe is a light-hearted part of many Christmas holiday celebrations, with some people looking forward to an innocent kiss, and some folks zealous to avoid getting caught under it.

Hang a sprig over a doorway everyone walks through and let the kissing and hilarity begin. One tradition says that each time a man kisses a woman under the mistletoe he must pick one berry from the sprig. When the berries are gone the kissing must end. Or . . . is it time to hang a fresh bunch of mistletoe?

Decorating for Love

BY TRISH BERG

Sometimes we look for love in all the wrong places. We think we can create love in our lives, make our lives more beautiful by plastering on decorations.

From evergreens to pine roping, and little white lights strung on every banister and doorway, I spend a lot of time decorating our house for the holidays. Building memories is what I like to call it. Things my children will remember twenty years from now with fondness and joy.

When we had a toddler and a baby, I tried a little too hard to "decorate" one Christmas. It all began when I saw a Hallmark commercial: a dad, missing his now adult daughter, walked to the top of a hill where they had gone every Christmas Eve when she was young. By moonlight, he opened the Christmas card she sent him.

I wanted to build memories like that on the two-hundred-acre farm where we lived. On Christmas Eve we'd decorate an evergreen that no one would see but us—decorating a tree for God's eyes only.

I bought strands of battery-operated white lights, tinsel, and ornaments, and spent hours stringing popcorn and cranberries so the animals could enjoy our gift to God. Now, in theory, this all sounded grand.

Then Christmas Eve arrived wrapped in a cold Ohio freeze. The wind chill zoomed below zero. My husband, Mike, gave me the look that said, "Are you sure about this?"

Yep. We're making memories—even if they include frostbite.

Too cold to hike, we drove our old Jeep, Lazarus, up the hill, our sweet girls swaddled like apple dumplings. On a steep hill in the woods, we found a lonely evergreen, all skinny and crooked. Just perfect.

Mike climbed out, stood on the hood of the Jeep, and began to drape the lights and garland. The girls and I remained in the car.

I watched. Sydney cried. Hannah shivered.

With a dying whoosh, the Jeep heater gave out. More chill seeped in. My nose turned ice-cube cold. Sydney's crying grew louder. On the hood, Mike looked like a cross between the abominable snowman and the Grinch.

With one final toss, he threw the remaining decorations toward the tree. He jumped into the Jeep, "I quit! Let's get back inside before we freeze to death."

Two babies crying, one parent frozen, one parent driving, we eased down the hill. I looked in the rearview mirror at our little evergreen with lumps and piles of lights here and there glowing in the night sky.

So much for perfection.

Back inside our home, I made hot cocoa. As we thawed, Mike and I looked at each other and laughed. And through that laughter we realized a very important life lesson: the true beauty of Christmas isn't in decorated trees or traditions. Christmas beauty lives in a bare stable where a baby was born without any decorating from me.

Over the years we discovered wonderful ways to celebrate Christmas. The difference is that I now let the love of God decorate our holidays. I don't rely on my efforts alone.

On that long ago Christmas Eve when we braved the Arctic blast to decorate our first outdoor tree, we spent too much time trying to create the perfect Christmas.

We forgot. God had already done that.

MORNING STAR LIGHT

Blessed are the meek, for they
will inherit the earth.

MATTHEW 5:5

WORD QUILTERS' WISDOM

In the fields, ponder a nighttime sky.
Imagine the hope the shepherds saw there.

CHAPTER FOUR

Homecoming

And everyone went to his own town to register. Luke 2:3

NOT EVERYONE CAN GO HOME FOR CHRISTMAS, BUT AN APARTMENT,
A CAR, A HOTEL ROOM, OR A TENT CAN BE HOME IF JESUS IS PRESENT.

Christmas in Kansas

BY CATHY MESSECAR

Our closet-size apartment seemed like Buckingham Palace. Even away from family and living on Army pay, we were king and queen. In a drafty old Kansas house, converted into living quarters, my husband, David, and I prepared to celebrate our first Christmas together. We'd reunited after his twelve months of Vietnam deployment. Our festive moods fit the joy-filled holidays.

That season our stockings overflowed with blessings—a Savior, new Kansas friends, and no more long-distance marriage. After a year and 9,300 miles of separation, we loved being within arm's reach.

In the making—a party for two. But our scraggly, barren tree looked like Charlie Brown's. The skeletal limbs needed sprucing. With only ten shopping days before Christmas, we planned to purchase our first tree decorations.

But on Shopping Saturday, we awoke to a paper-white snowy outdoors, three reams deep. Twelve inches of snow made motorized travel treacherous. Young and determined, we bundled into our warmest clothing for a two-mile trek to a store. Making do, I strapped my husband's size 12 combat boots on my size 7 feet.

As South Texans, used to barefooted walks on hot Galveston beaches, the delicate particles of frozen fluff delighted us. A couple of hearty souls were out in their toasty warm vehicles, but no one else was afoot. On our hike, we assisted a few stranded motorists by pushing skidded cars out of snowdrifts.

Trudging toward the store, Dave held my gloved hand and tugged me along. By the time we arrived, the combat boots felt like heavy anchors. With visions of red and green ornaments, I clumped toward the holiday aisle. Scenes of a *Better Homes and Gardens* Christmas played in my mind.

Eyes aglow, I found the holiday trinkets. The spectrum of celebratory colors narrowed. In vain, I searched for just one box of red ornaments. Only two colors remained on the shelves: gold and pink. Pink for a soldier's first Christmas tree?

We settled for several boxes of pastel decorations. Charlie Brown's tree would be plentiful with Pepto-Bismol-hued ornaments. Too exhausted to trim the tree after tramping home, we opted for naps. By nightfall we strung lights and with care hung the glass orbs. The evergreen switched personalities. Standing sentry, a frilly Shirley Temple tree saluted the season.

In 1968, although our families were far away and we'd not found traditional red and green decorations, we were grateful because God granted our prayers. We were together.

This year as we deck the family room, we'll reminisce about our first Christmas. Pink is good. Combat boots tramping on home soil is really good. Together, we'll hang many memory tokens on the boughs of our Christmas tree, and we'll find a special branch for the remaining two pastel ornaments.

BETHLEHEM STAR

The Word became flesh and blood,
and moved into the neighborhood.
We saw the glory with our own eyes,
the one-of-a-kind glory,
like Father, like Son,
Generous inside and out,
true from start to finish.

JOHN 1:14 THE MESSAGE

GINGERBREAD GENEALOGY

Las Posadas ~ Search for an Inn ~ TERRA HANGEN

In Mexico, children carry candles and walk from house to house in neighborhoods in late December, reenacting Mary and Joseph's search for a room in an inn or posada. Mexican Americans brought this beautiful ceremony, "Las Posadas," to the United States.

People dressed as Joseph and Mary lead children to visit houses chosen in advance. Sometimes Mary rides on a burro. Adults lead children in the singing of Christmas hymns as they search for the houses on their route. At each home, the group follows Joseph's singing: "*En nombre de cielo,*" or "In the name of heaven, I ask you for posada, for my beloved wife can walk no more."

People in the houses turn the pilgrims away as planned, and sing in answer: "This is not an inn, keep walking. I will not open, you might be a thief." The Holy Pilgrims are refused refuge until the final house is reached, when the innkeeper sings, "Posada I give to you, Holy Pilgrims, and I beg your pardon, I had not recognized you."

Participants know people at this house have prepared a party. Pilgrims and the folk in this welcoming house sing "*Entren Santos Peregrinos . . . mi corazon*" or "Enter Holy Pilgrims . . . my heart." The pilgrims enter for a celebration, where they eat food such as tamales and drink hot chocolate. For the festive finale to Las Posadas, a piñata is broken open revealing nuts, fruit, and hard candy.

We sate among the stalls at Bethlehem;

The dumb kine from their fodder turning them,

Softened their horned faces

To almost human gazes

Toward the newly Born:

The simple shepherds from the star-lit brooks

Brought their visionary looks,

As yet in their astonied hearing rung

The strange sweet angel-tonge:

The magi of the East, in sandals worn,

Knelt reverent, sweeping round,

With long pale beards, their gifts upon the ground,

The incense, myrrh, and gold

These baby hands were impotent to hold:

So let all earthlies and celestials wait

Upon thy royal state

Sleep, sleep, my kingly One.—

THE HOLY NIGHT
BY ELIZABETH BARRETT BROWNING

A FEW OF OUR FAVORITE THINGS
Favorite Homemade Food Gifts

BRENDA ~ Peppermint Kisses

CATHY ~ Cherry Biscotti

KAREN ~ Apple Butter

LESLIE ~ Petite Banana Bread Loaves

TERRA ~ Sugared Nut Variety

TRISH ~ Sand Art Brownies

STOCKING STUFFER TRADITIONS
Jigsaw Puzzles ~ LESLIE WILSON

Early in December set up a card table and chairs. Put
out a jigsaw puzzle for family members to work
on throughout the holidays. Does your family
like competition? Keep a record of how
many pieces each member matches.

E dward Hibbard Johnson (1846-1917), vice president of Edison Electric Company, first trimmed his holiday tree with electric Christmas lights on December 22, 1882, in New York City. The hand-wired lights honored his friend and associate Thomas Edison. Those first lights were walnut in size and shone in the patriotic colors of red, white, and blue. By the 1900s, stores began lighting their holiday display windows with colored lights, but they were too expensive for the average American. General Electric first offered Christmas lamps for sale or rent in a *Scientific American Magazine* ad on November 28, 1900.

Modern LED lights use about 90% less energy than traditional incandescent lights. They are safer since the bulbs are only warm to the touch, even after several hours of use.

PEPPERMINTS FOR LITTLE ONES

Christmas Snack Jar Gift ~ Karen Robbins

Even two- and three-year-olds can help assemble these snacks for hard-to-buy-for adults. For each pint jar: ¼ cup M & M candies (green and red), ½ cup honey roasted peanuts, ¼ cup raisins, and 1 cup Honey Nut Cheerios cereal. Layer ingredients in jars. Decorate lids with holiday stickers, ribbons or bells. Write these instructions on a self-stick label: Empty contents into bowl. Toss to mix. Enjoy!

Baklava ~ Terra Hangen

Baklava is a favorite dessert in Turkey and Greece, and in my house. I first encountered it while attending college in Istanbul, Turkey. It is possible to hand make fillo dough, a time consuming process, but fortunately store-bought dough is available.

Greek husbands brag that "my wife makes fillo so thin that I can read a newspaper through it." I made this recipe for a church potluck, prompting a man to shout across the room, "I want to marry the woman who made this."

fillo (phyllo) dough, 16 ounces	¼ cup sugar
1 stick unsalted butter (½ cup)	½ cup honey
16 oz. finely chopped walnuts or pistachios	1 tsp. cinnamon
1 glass dish 9 x 13 inches, 1 pastry brush	

Thaw fillo in refrigerator overnight. On kitchen counter bring it to room temperature. Unfold dough. To prevent dough from drying, cover it with a damp (not wet) towel and plastic wrap. Melt the butter and preheat the oven to 325°.

Brush inside of dish with butter. Set in two or three layers of fillo, brush with butter. Continue layers of fillo brushed with butter for about twenty layers, roughly half the sheets. Fold over the edges of fillo if larger than dish. Mix sugar, cinnamon and nuts, sprinkle over twentieth fillo layer.

Continue adding the rest of fillo and brushing every two or three layers with butter. Top with a layer or two of fillo, brush the top with butter. Before cooking, use a sharp knife to cut through all layers (a diamond pattern). Bake for about 50 minutes until golden brown. While hot, pour honey on top. Cool before serving.

A GIFT FOR YOU

Home Scents ~ CATHY MESSECAR

To scent your home without using aerosols,
simmer spices—cinnamon, cloves, nutmeg, or
allspice—in several cups of water. Use jarred,
fresh-ground or whole. A side benefit: the
gentle steam will humidify the air.

EVERGREEN THUMB

Amaryllis ~ TERRA HANGEN

Even if you don't claim a green thumb, you can grow spectacular Amaryllis flowers that bloom at Christmas. From bulbs as large as a fist, Amaryllis produce flowers up to eight inches across on tall, sturdy stems.

Most Amaryllis will bloom in six to eight weeks, so plant bulbs about October 25. Buy a ceramic pot slightly bigger than the bulb. My pot is eighteen inches around and five inches tall. The pot must have a drainage hole. Put in a bit of potting soil and plant the bulb pointed side up, leaving it one-third uncovered.

For beauty, place gardener marbles on top of the soil. Set the pot in a sunny window, water once a week, and watch for stalks to sprout. Rotate the pot to keep the stalks growing straight.

The Clown, also called Candy Cane, has bold red and white flowers and blooms in six to eight weeks. Matterhorn bulbs produce white flowers and bloom in a mere four to six weeks. Bulbs may be purchased at most garden centers.

A Twice-Shared Christmas

BY LINDA LaMAR JEWELL

All I wanted for Christmas was to share it with my husband, Jim, and my son, Ty. In years past, the three of us laughed and enjoyed the holiday together. Instead of being together as a family, this was the first Christmas my son would spend overseas in the military.

The afternoon of December 24, Jim and I drove in silence to Albuquerque's Old Town. My heart ached too much to talk. How would Ty spend Christmas Day? Had he returned safely from a war zone to his base in Germany? Would he pull guard duty? If he had the day off, would he spend it alone?

While offering up a heartsick prayer, I latched onto a stray thought. Although my son was eight time zones away, I could still find a way to share this Christmas Eve with both him and my husband. I wouldn't ruin my Christmas with Jim just because Ty wasn't here. Instead, I'd share it in the present moment with Jim—and with Ty later in a letter.

After Jim parked the car, I jumped out and pulled on my purple coat. I slipped my fingers into my husband's warm hand as we ambled through Old Town. A sense of purpose loosed my tongue and I chatted about the adventure that lay before us. I felt upbeat, on-task, ready to experience and record a vibrant Christmas Eve message.

At first I noticed the excitement and wonder on the faces of other wanderers. My smiles received greetings from children and grins from adults. Twinkling eyes accompanied the gracious nod of an elderly gentleman.

Jim and I stopped outside a shop to listen to sweet refrains. I spied the singer—wrapped in a fur coat, hat, and muff—on the balcony. With my eyes lifted up, I allowed her to write the old words of joy on my renewed heart. While we listened to the carols, late afternoon quickly slipped into twilight. As the sun set and the temperature fell, I pulled on my red cap and gloves.

Jim and I moved on toward the Plaza outlined with *luminarios*—stubby white candles secured in sand at the bottom of small brown paper bags—set out to light the way of the Christ Child. Like the stars above, they were lit one by one, and together they mirrored the Milky Way canopy overhead. Hundreds, perhaps thousands, of *luminarios* outlined the Plaza, perched on adobe walls and flat rooftops, the gazebo and sidewalks.

We followed the lit path to the old adobe church. Filled with people, we squeezed through doors festooned with evergreens. Like worshipers in centuries past, we listened again to the ageless story of the Messiah. Next, we walked across the street and climbed white wooden steps to watch the crowd mingle and swirl below us at the food stand selling fresh Indian fry bread.

After making the rounds of Old Town's Plaza, we crossed the avenue into the Country Club area. Again, *luminarios* outlined street after street. Along the golf fairway, twenty-six tethered hot air balloons glowed like a giant string of multicolored Christmas lights. A young couple wore light strips around their necks, and a policeman directed traffic from a motorcycle adorned with a large blinking star.

Strains of classical music filled the air, and I stood enchanted at a Currier & Ives scene of a bay window Christmas tree, complete with twinkling lights and colored glass decorations.

Moving on, we turned a corner into a scene from Charles Dickens' time, complete with a haze of pungent cedar smoke. Well-wishers crowded the streets. Clip-clops heralded a horse-drawn buggy from which passengers threw candy canes to the crowd.

Several hours later, Jim and I wandered back through Old Town where we stopped at a restaurant and sat near the fireplace to sip cinnamon-spiced cider. While I warmed my toes and nose, I noticed a tree—complete with decorations and gifts—hanging upside down from the ceiling.

My heart was overfull with sights, sounds, touches, tastes, and smells I shared with Jim.

Later at home—before I turned in for that night—I recorded the details of that Christmas Eve in a letter to Ty.

The first year Ty was stationed overseas, God answered my heartsick prayer. I shared Christmas Eve with my family the only way I could—in real time and the same space with my husband—and across time and miles with my son.

MORNING STAR LIGHT

Here I am! I stand at the door and knock.
If anyone hears my voice and opens the door, I will
come in to him and eat with him, and he with me.

REVELATION 3:20

WORD QUILTERS' WISDOM

Kindness refuels others.
Make your home a replenishing place.

CHAPTER FIVE

Holiday Hospitality

She wrapped him in cloths and placed him in a manger,
because there was no room for them in the inn. LUKE 2:7

CHRISTMAS COMMERCIALS SHOW HAPPY FAMILIES. IN REAL LIFE, SOME ARE HURTING DURING THE
HOLIDAY SEASON. EXTEND HOSPITALITY TO THOSE WHO ARE ALONE OR MAY BE OVERLOOKED.

FAMILY SNAPSHOT

Mr. Paul

BY BRENDA NIXON

On a frosty December morning, I talked with my daughters, Lynsey and Laura,
and reminded them how God gave an undeserved gift, the hope offered
through the birth of Christ.

I suggested that we do a special family project to underscore the message of
Christmas. Even though they were children, I urged them to think about selfless giving
with no expectation to receive, "God uses servants of all ages."

Lynsey, then fifteen, popped up with, "We can make a gift basket for one of the old people at church!" Living with a teen had taught me to seize and rally around any act of outward thoughtfulness, so I encouraged her idea.

Nine-year-old Laura chimed in, "Yeah, we can put stuff together and give it to 'em for Christmas." We agreed that a surprise gift basket would be our family project.

"Now who'll be our recipient?" I asked. Laura suggested several names of senior citizens at church. After much discussion, we settled on "Mr. Paul." Paul Untirkircher was a cheerful, kind, rotund gent. He and his wife had a long, loving marriage but no children. Mr. Paul, as he was known in our home, had no living family. Each Sunday he and his wife faithfully worked in the church's sound booth recording services for the homebound. They felt it was their ministry. They also felt it was their ministry to "hush" the children chattering in the hall. And often they were the eyes and ears of absent parents.

But early that year Mr. Paul's wife received a diagnosis of terminal cancer. Within months, his world changed as he buried his wife and partner of fifty years. We knew it'd be a particularly lonely Christmas for him.

Parties, shopping, rehearsals, baking, and festive dinners filled the weeks following our family project discussion. Even through the demanding schedule, we each thought of Mr. Paul.

Lynsey found an attractive basket large enough to hold a multitude of tiny treasures including lip balm, aftershave, and a package of chocolate truffles. While baking, we set aside homemade cookies and candy for Mr. Paul. On shopping trips, Laura found numerous keepsakes and eyes twinkling, said, "Mr. Paul will like this!"

Then we added her chosen gift to our shopping cart. Lynsey made a Christmas card, and Dad suggested gifts from a man's point of view: a tie, devotional book, and wallet. Together we came up with a variety of presents to pack in our gift basket. We imagined Mr. Paul's reaction.

Lynsey thought he'd cry.

Laura said he'd laugh.

The time spent focusing on another person gave me multiple opportunities to remind my girls of God's gift to us—how satisfied God was in giving of His treasure. As our basket and anticipation swelled, my girls began arguing over which one would offer it. After we included our final treats, Laura cheerfully decorated the basket. Her homemade bow and carefully placed tissue paper made it a beautiful gift.

The Sunday before Christmas arrived. Our eager family gently carried the bulging basket into church. Lynsey and Laura both held onto the handle. My husband and I followed close behind.

Mr. Paul sat in his small, glass-enclosed cubicle turning knobs on a complex control panel. The girls stumbled over each other in their enthusiasm to climb the two steps to his level. Hearing the commotion, he turned towards them. When his eyes fell on the basket my girls shouted, "Merry Christmas!" and shoved it in his direction.

With a look of genuine surprise, he reached out to accept our gift. His aged arms cradled it as tears welled up in his blue eyes. For a moment, words failed him, but he spoke volumes through his grateful expression. A gift given. A gift received.

With fondness my girls still remember that first family project when we honored Jesus, and the Christmas message came alive in their hearts.

BETHLEHEM STAR

[So] he got up from the meal . . . wrapped a towel around his waist. After that, he poured water into a basin and began to wash his disciples' feet.

JOHN 13:4-5

GINGERBREAD GENEALOGY

Christmas Cards ~ LESLIE WILSON

Christmas Cards began as "schoolpieces," written by schoolboys in England, greetings to their parents and proof of their handwriting progress. Next came "Christmas pieces," simple pen-and-ink designs hand-drawn on a sheet of paper.

Then, in 1843, J.C. Horsley designed the first formal card, a Christmas scene framed in three panels: the center was a homey table scene; the two sides depicted Christmas charity—feeding the hungry and clothing the naked. The card was "lithographed on a stiff, dark cardboard," according to Tristan Coffin in *The Book of Christmas Folklore*. The card read, "A Merry Christmas and a Happy New Year to you." One thousand were printed, and one sent to a James Peters still survives.

In England in the late 1800s, mail cost only a penny to send, so the custom of sending Christmas cards became popular. This tradition continues to grow. Americans send more than two billion cards each year. And Christmas E-cards can be sent to

VINTAGE POETRY

Do all the good you can,
By all the means you can,
In all the ways you can,
In all the places you can,
At all the times you can,
To all the people you can,
As long as ever you can.

BY JOHN WESLEY (1703-1791)

A GIFT FOR YOU

Less is Best ~ LESLIE WILSON AND CATHY MESSECAR

Tell children they will receive three gifts each, the same number as the wise men brought to baby Jesus. Help adults avoid life-clutter by choosing gifts that can be used within a year: a calendar, soaps, stationery, candles, fruit, teas and coffees, a book of postage stamps, or gift certificates for services such as oil changes.

A FEW OF OUR FAVORITE THINGS
Most Outrageous Gift Given

BRENDA

I named a star after each of my daughters and a galaxy for my friend's daughter on her 16th birthday. (Commercial companies who name stars present recipients with certificates as symbolic gestures. The International Astronomical Union [IAU] alone has the right to name stars. The star-count is indefinite, and most are only given identifying numbers.)

CATHY

Early in our marriage, my husband competed in a farm sport, tractor pulling. He found a motor for his lightweight tractor, but thought we couldn't afford it. I talked to the owner, and we worked out an engine-layaway plan. I didn't gift wrap the motor—the shape might have spoiled the surprise. Besides, the motor outsized our tree. In a Christmas note, my husband learned of his gift.

KAREN

When the "Horseshoe," the Ohio State University football stadium, made the temporary south stands permanent, they sold engraved bricks for use in new walkways outside the stadium—the answer to my Christmas dilemma that year. My husband, an avid Buckeye fan, received a card and picture of his brick, his name and graduation dates written on it. Each year we search it out among the thousands of other Buckeye fans who received the same honor.

LESLIE

I asked my sister, who is in advertising, to create a logo for my husband, and then I surprised him with shirts and ball caps with the logo embroidered on them. He wears them and gives them away to clients. He said they're the best gift he's ever received.

TERRA

At age seven, I selected my dad's Christmas gift, a pretty green glass ashtray. It didn't dawn on me that Daddy didn't smoke. When Dad opened it, he exclaimed how much he liked it. He filled it with paper clips and put it in the top drawer of his writing desk. Each year I travel a thousand miles to visit. He still has the same desk, and in the drawer—the green glass ashtray—the gift accepted with love and without a hint of criticism.

TRISH

For busy mothers of preschoolers—girlfriends, neighbors, daughters-in-law, sisters—gift them with A DAY OFF OF MOTHERHOOD certificate. Limit this to six unless you know a mother of septuplets! Print coupon: MERRY CHRISTMAS – Entitles you to one DAY OFF OF MOTHERHOOD. Phone to schedule a date. Drop off your children at 9:00 a.m. and pick them up at 5:00 p.m. Go shopping, get your hair done, or go home to nap.

TRIVIA TREASURES

(L)ester and Edyta Szladewski said hospitality is extended in Poland by setting an extra plate at their Christmas dinner table—a family of five will have six place settings. This place of honor is reserved for unexpected guests. A candle or light in a home window signals that an extra plate is set for the homeless or wanderer needing a Christmas meal.

COOKIE CANISTER

Chocolate-Orange Sandies ~ CATHY MESSECAR

1 cup butter (2 sticks or ½ pound)
1 ¾ cups all-purpose flour
1 ¼ cups confectioner's sugar
¼ cup unsweetened cocoa

1 cup finely chopped pecans
1 tsp. orange extract
1 tsp. orange zest

Preheat oven to 400° F. In large bowl, mix butter, flour, one cup of confectioner's sugar, cocoa, pecans, and extract until blended. Roll into one inch balls and place onto ungreased cookie pan. Bake for 8-10 minutes, or until set. Allow to cool. Roll in confectioner's sugar. Store cookies in airtight container. Yield: 4 dozen.

PEPPERMINTS FOR LITTLE ONES

Candle Light ~ LESLIE WILSON

Several times in December, eat evening meals by candlelight. An alternative—with only the Christmas tree lights on, spread a blanket and have a picnic nearby. The soft lighting will usher calm into your household after a busy day.

STOCKING STUFFER TRADITION

Heritage Tablecloth ~ CATHY MESSECAR

To help my family recall blessings, I provide a light-colored, tight woven tablecloth (padded underneath) and permanent marking pens. I encourage every age family member and guests to sign the tablecloth.

Our tablecloth, in use for eight years, has Callie's and Wendy's engagement announcement inside a red heart. Jack, when a kindergartner, wrote the whole alphabet along the edge while adults ate dessert. Age 6, Adam drew fanciful turkeys.

When I retire the tablecloth, I'll make a booklet of names, notes, and dates, so each family can have one. Our family history is on the tablecloth in drawings of food, outlines of preschoolers' hands, and infant Jolie's footprint. The Savior, pie, chocolate, drums, and trucks—all are listed as thanksgivings. My sweet mother-in-law, Nancy, gathered all the sentiments in her 2002 message: "I'm thankful for the gifts of life here on earth and the heavens above."

EVERGREEN THUMB

Pine Cone Wreath ~ TERRA HANGEN

Materials: pine cones, grape vine base, craft wire. Optional: spray paint, wire edged ribbon, glitter, and glue.

Gather pine cones and dry the cones in a warm place indoors for a few days or buy cones from a craft store. A grape vine wreath provides the base. Weave your own from pruned vines, purchase from a hobby shop, or buy a used wreath at a thrift shop.

Next, cut 18-inch lengths of craft wire, wrap one around the base of each pine cone, twist to secure. Use wire ends to attach pine cones to base. Cluster cones at top or bottom or fill the entire wreath with cones. Wreath can be spray painted with a splash of white, bronze, or a color that complements your décor. For a sparkly effect, apply glue and sprinkle on glitter. Add festive wire-edged ribbon, jingle bells, holly berries, or other trimmings.

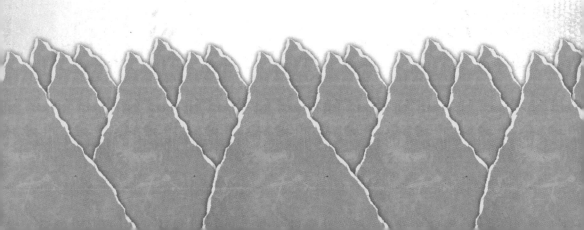

Five Boxes of Christmas Cards

BY JEANETTE SHARP

I bolted for the door. The last bell in Mrs. Mitchell's fifth grade class rang that afternoon in November, 1954. Outside, the overcast sky and the chill in the air sent shivers up my skinny bare legs. I hurried home to get a snack and pick up my cardboard carrying case with boxed Christmas cards—my first try at door-to-door selling.

I headed out with high hopes and knocked on every door for blocks but found no buyers. The North wind turned cold and my teeth chattered as it blew a gale through the thin hand-me-down coat. My chapped lips burned and my hands numbed, frozen to the handles of the case. The urge to give up and go home mounted. My once high hopes sagged.

In the past, my twin sister, Annette, and our little brother, Stuart, went with Grandma Hudson to Uncle Glen's groves where we picked up pecans to earn money for Christmas. This year I needed to earn way more money. Times had changed at our house.

Daddy had died in May that year. It happened on a Friday. When Annette and I walked home for lunch, we spotted his huge dump truck parked in front of our house and ran the rest of the way. Mother met us at the door. "Shush, your daddy's asleep and doesn't feel good." Daddy never got sick. We peeked into the bedroom and watched him sleep for a minute, before heading back to school.

At 4:30, we ran home from school and followed close on Mother's heels when she went in to check on him. She couldn't make him wake up. "Oh, goodness," she said. With a scared look in her eyes, she phoned Dr. Daily. He came right away dressed in his usual brown suit, a striped tie and a brown hat. His kind voice, full of assurance gave us hope, but he couldn't wake up Daddy either. He told Mother a heart attack took him.

Later, I worried about our money and could tell Mother did, too. I often saw her fight back tears. She wrote down everything she spent in a little black book and let me see how she kept a record of our expenses. Christmas would be bleak without Daddy. Oh, how we needed him.

My hopes dimmed that late afternoon—I still had all five boxes in my carrying case. I decided to try one more door. I walked up the driveway, knocked on the door, and whispered, "Oh God, please help me sell all five boxes." The bigness of my prayer seemed almost unreasonable.

The lady of the house answered the door right away, and I showed her my wares. Interested, she knelt down to see them. After a careful look, she asked the price, then straightened. "I'll take all five boxes." I could hardly believe my ears!

All of a sudden, nothing mattered—not what Mother's little black book said, the cold North wind, or my hand-me-down coat. Clutching the money, I ran home to tell everyone. We had always gone to church, and I believed in God. But this was the first time I knew through and through in my heart God heard me, saw me, and cared for me.

MORNING STAR LIGHT

The King will reply, 'I tell you the truth, whatever you did for one of the least of these brothers of mine, you did for me.'

MATTHEW 25:40

WORD QUILTERS' WISDOM
Holiday "orphans" abound.
Adopt the abandoned.

CHAPTER SIX

Celebrate

An angel of the Lord appeared . . . "I bring you good news of great joy that will be for all the people. Today in the town of David a Savior has been born to you; he is Christ the Lord." LUKE 2:9-11

TREES, TINSEL, AND PRETTY WRAPPED PRESENTS ADD SPARKLE TO CHRISTMAS, BUT THE TRUE SOURCE OF LIGHT AND JOY IS THE SAVIOR—THE ONE WHO EXPERIENCED FAMILY LAUGHTER AND GIGGLES WHILE ON EARTH, THE SAME SOUNDTRACKS OF LOVING FAMILIES TODAY.

FAMILY SNAPSHOT

Be in Good Health

BY CATHY MESSECAR

We expected an ordinary evening, but Daddy brought home a surprise.

In my childhood home mid-December, the aroma of vegetable stew filled the kitchen while my family waited for Daddy to come home from work. My sister Sherry and I set the table. My younger brother Kenny, age four, played underneath. Mother, of the stay-at-home variety, put the finishing touches on the evening meal.

My parents lived the American Dream. Daddy, a union metal-lather, moved his family to Houston, Texas, in 1957. They bought their first home and furnishings, and Mother painted walls and sewed curtains, transforming the two-bedroom, one-bath frame house into a cozy cottage.

Previously in Arkansas, we lived in rental houses and moved frequently to reside near Dad's work. The permanent move to Texas brought stability and a host of first-time experiences. We worshiped at the same church each Sunday. Dad bought a home air conditioner to temper the humid coastal air. We acquired a television. Pets were now allowed—kittens purred on the back steps, a caged canary serenaded, and goldfish swam circles in a large round bowl.

That evening, in the chartreuse kitchen, the table set with pink and green Fiesta Ware, we waited for the familiar sound of Dad's truck. The recognizable thump of tires driving onto two concrete runners of the driveway sent us scurrying to the window. In dim twilight, we saw Daddy get out and stretch. He pushed his cap back from his forehead with his index finger causing the bill to tilt skyward—an endearing habit.

Then Daddy reached into his truck for his metal lunch box and thermos, but he also drew out a brown paper bag. What did he have in the sack?

In seconds, the back door to the kitchen opened. Daddy tossed his cap onto a peg. He gave Mother a squeeze and kiss, then bent down to exchange kisses with his three children.

Depositing his gear and the mysterious sack onto the white-tiled kitchen counter, he said, "Give me time to wash up and we'll eat. Oh . . . and I have a surprise for you kids." He whispered something in Mother's ear. She smiled.

He left to clean up, but his announcement jump-started the jitters. We knew he'd revealed the secret to Mother. We begged, "What's in the sack?"

"Wait and see." Mom sent us on Dad's heels, "Help your brother wash his hands for supper."

We passed through the living room with little Kenny in tow. Near the turquoise sectional stood our Christmas tree decked with finery. The mysterious brown bag in the kitchen held as much mystique as the array of packages nestled underneath.

Back in the kitchen with the family seated at the Formica-topped table, I wiggled in my seat. What's Daddy's surprise? After grace, my sister and I peppered Dad with questions. He seemed to enjoy ignoring them, and I noticed more secretive smiles pass between Daddy and Mother.

The meal over, Sherry and I cleared dishes, and Daddy asked me to bring his thermos and the paper bag to the table. He asked Sherry to get five coffee cups. My sister and I looked at each other in amazement. Would we be allowed after dinner coffee, the adult ritual?

With everyone seated, Daddy uncapped his thermos. He poured a cup for Mother, and then did the same for all of us. Dad lifted his cup and said, "It's wassail."

I sniffed the misty vapor rising from my cup. Hmmm. It smelled like pumpkin pie. Then, Daddy opened the paper sack and took out three gingerbread men with raisin eyes. They matched his palm in size.

"At Bank of Southwest where I'm remodeling, they serve wassail and gingerbread men and have a choir. I asked to bring some wassail and cookies home to you kids."

The heady spices of cloves and cinnamon settled in the kitchen. I took a sip of the golden brew. The perfect blend of fruit juices and spices enslaved my taste buds. I fell in love. The gingerbread—yummy—but what intrigued me was my first taste of wassail.

Later, as a young adult, I worked at Citizens State Bank in Houston where I couriered to other financial giants. Bank of Southwest, on my route, continued its tradition of serving snacks and hosting a "singing Christmas tree," and I again enjoyed wassail and gingerbread and thought back to my first taste in my parents' kitchen.

Many years later, in my own home, my sister phoned. Excited, she told me a newspaper printed the famed bank's wassail recipe. She recited it while I scribbled ingredients on a piece of tissue paper.

Now, on a morning near Christmas, I pull out the recipe, measure apple cider, lemon, and orange juice, and drop one cinnamon stick and a few cloves into a pan. On the range top, the Old Norse concoction simmers. Flavors mingle. I ladle the brew into my ruby red mug and think pleasant thoughts toward friends, "Be in good health."

With my first sip, memories flood in—of Daddy, Mother, a chartreuse kitchen, and a work thermos filled with wassail.

(Wassail is pronounced "WAHS-uhl" from *Ves heill*, Norse for "be in good health.")

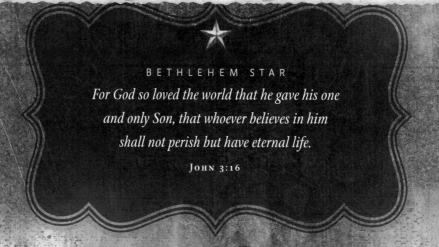

BETHLEHEM STAR

*For God so loved the world that he gave his one
and only Son, that whoever believes in him
shall not perish but have eternal life.*

JOHN 3:16

GINGERBREAD GENEALOGY

Giving Gifts ~ LESLIE WILSON

Though the wise men gave gifts to Christ—not one another—we give gifts to each other to commemorate and celebrate Jesus' birth. Giving gifts is not rooted in the pagan practice of astrology as some maintain. This misconception came from the notion that "Magi," in the original Greek, referred to "astrologers." However, history shows that the Magi who came to visit Jesus were not merely stargazers but were well learned in the arts and sciences of their day. The translation "wise men" is more accurate.

Hank Hanegraaff, in his article "Is Christmas Christian?" notes, "Obviously our risen, reigning Redeemer doesn't need a thing. However, when we give to one another, Christ considers that as good as 'giving unto Him'" (Matthew 25:37-40).

Some old-fashioned gift traditions include a present of confections to ensure sweetness for the year to come. Further blessing-gifts for recipients might include lamps for light and warmth or money signifying a plentiful year. The wise men brought myrrh, frankincense, and gold to the baby Jesus, and at Christmas, the wise still know that it's "more blessed to give than to receive" (Acts 20:35).

VINTAGE LYRICS

Heap on more wood! the wind is chill;
But let it whistle as it will,
We'll keep our Christmas merry still,
We'll keep our Christmas merry still,
Each age has deem'd the new-born year
The fittest time for festal cheer;
And well our Christian sires of old
Lov'd when the year its course had roll'd

BY SIR WALTER SCOTT (1771-1832)

STOCKING STUFFER TRADITION

Christmas Mail ~ LESLIE WILSON

At the family dining table, place the Christmas greeting
cards you receive in a basket. Before the dinnertime
prayer, let family members take turns opening
cards. Explain your relationship to the giver
and then pray for the families.

TRIVIA TREASURE

Interested in seeing the North Pole? Try a spring visit and participate in the North Pole Marathon. Adventurers brave sub-zero weather to run or walk the frozen Arctic surface. A mere 6-12 feet of ice separates runners from the very chilly Arctic Ocean. From around the globe, athletes gather for this grueling test of skills. The Arctic surface is in continuous motion due to the flow of the ocean current beneath, but runners don't feel the sensation of movement. Accommodations: heated tents.

In 2007, Thomas Maguire, from Ireland, completed the 26.2 mile course in a record time of three hours, 36 minutes and 10 seconds, among a field of 43 athletes from 22 nations.

PEPPERMINTS FOR LITTLE ONES

Bedtime Stories ~ LESLIE WILSON

*Start a collection of Christmas books and add
to it each year. At bedtime during the
month of December, read them to children.*

A FEW OF OUR FAVORITE THINGS
Favorite Gifts Received

BRENDA

Two Christmases ago, intensely low about my career, I wondered if I should continue with my writing, quit, or move to a remote farm and raise llamas. Under the tree that year, my husband placed his gift for me—a threadbare, 1942 copy of *Cross Creek* by Marjorie Kinnan Rawlings. Perhaps during a period of artistic frustration, she moved from New York City to a "bend in the country road," where she wrote, "We need above all, I think, a certain remoteness from urban confusion."

She persisted in her craft, and wrote about the "very simple things" at the Creek. A New York publisher bought the manuscript and, eventually, *Cross Creek* sold to movie rights. This gift told me that my husband "got it" – he felt my inner argument, and Rawling's remarkable strong will was my impetus to keep writing. At Christmas two years later, I had two book contracts.

CATHY

After losing the diamond from my engagement ring in Murfreesboro, Arkansas—home of the only diamond mine in the USA—I asked my husband, David, for a simple gold band. Santa Dave gifted me with the perfect wedding band on Christmas Morning, and several years later, on Valentine's Day, the engagement ring sparkled to life again.

KAREN

My husband, Bob, gave me a trip to Williamsburg, Virginia and also made arrangements for grandparents to care for our children during the trip. While in Williamsburg, we saw traditional Christmas decorations, enjoyed a Christmas feast, and learned how to decorate in colonial Williamsburg style.

LESLIE

My parents and my husband teamed up to send me to my first big writer conference—Mount Hermon, in the Santa Cruz Mountains of California. They knew how important it was for me to experience that, but I had no income as a writer. Their gift started me on a career as a speaker, humor columnist, and freelance writer. The resulting income has helped me attend a major conference every year since.

TERRA

During a visit to my hometown, I picked out fifty family slides from thousands that document our family history. My husband and I had the slides transferred to a CD. One of the slides, taken in 1944, is only the slightest bit faded and has an ethereal beauty, showing the tenderness between my mom and dad.

For Christmas, my husband printed two photos from that slide for me and my sister. I love to gaze at the photograph and imagine the time when my parents were newlyweds and their world was full of promise.

TRISH

My husband, Mike, gave the gift of volunteer help. Our 4th child was due in early January, and after Christmas break, I would have three older children to get ready for school every morning and a new baby. Mike arranged for dear women from our church to come over every morning of the workweek at 6:00 a.m. to help with the morning routine. Over a half dozen faithful women volunteered to be on our Mom Squad and became part of my best Christmas gift ever.

A Dunkin' Cookie ~ Cathy Messecar

This recipe is from Aunt Margaret Johnson. These firm cookies are yummy for dunkin' in milk or coffee. Rolls of dough can be kept in refrigerator to bake up quick treats for pop-in guests. Add optional ingredients to create different flavors.

6 cups flour	Optional—mix and match additions
4 tsp. baking powder	⅓ cup coconut
½ tsp. salt	⅓ cup dried fruit, chopped
1 ½ cups shortening	⅓ cup chopped nuts
1 cup brown sugar	½ tsp. cinnamon
2 cups granulated sugar	¼ tsp. nutmeg
2 eggs well beaten	⅓ cup mini chocolate chips
2 tsp. vanilla	½ tsp. orange extract, ½ tsp. orange zest

Sift flour, salt, and baking powder together. In a very large bowl, cream shortening and sugar until fluffy. Add eggs and vanilla. Mix well. Add dry ingredients.

Divide dough into six portions. Leave plain or flavor with options. Shape portions into cylinder-shaped rolls. Wrap each in clear plastic. Chill in refrigerator until firm or freeze for later use. Cut into ½-inch slices and bake on greased cookie sheet. Bake at 375° for 8-10 minutes. Yield: 6-8 dozen

EVERGREEN THUMB

Living Christmas Tree ~ Terra Hangen

Create a Christmas legacy for your family by planting a living Christmas tree in your yard. For families with plenty of available land, plant a tree each year and name them for special people, like "Nona's tree."

Enjoy your decorated, living tree as the star of your home for a week before planting it. Before purchasing a living tree, consider the full height this tiny tree will reach. Noble Fir, Grand Fir, and White Pine are classic Christmas trees that can live 100 years and reach 60 to 90 feet tall, with branch spreads up to 30 feet. Is a tree this size appropriate for your yard or acreage?

For typical yards, dwarf Blue Spruce cultivars are excellent choices, with perfect conical shapes and thick foliage. Fat Albert reaches fifteen feet and Blaukissen or Blue Kiss reaches eight feet tall, in zones 2 to 7. The conifer Chamaecyparis obtusa Compacta reaches ten feet tall, and Aurea 20 feet tall, in zones 5-8. Evergreens need full sun and well-drained soil. If soil freezes in your area, dig a planting hole in the fall, and fill it with leaves.

Before placing your living Christmas tree in your home, keep the tree in an unheated garage or on a porch for a few days to let it acclimate to the warmer temperature of your house. Trees need cool temperatures, so keep them indoors for only a week, with plenty of light, and away from heaters or fireplaces. Keep the roots moist but not standing in water. Before planting outdoors, put the tree back on the porch or in the garage for a few days.

A GIFT FOR YOU

Build a Manger ~ Trish Berg

For a family project, enlist Dad, Mom, and kids to build a manger.

Christmas 1992, our first as husband and wife, we had no money and decided not to exchange gifts. Secretly, Mike made a wooden manger out of old barn siding with hay glued inside. Crooked and cracked, it looked ancient like I imagined the original feeding trough.

Each Christmas since, he buys a figurine for the crèche. When we unpack Christmas decorations each year, the manger is the one my four children are most eager to display. They play with it throughout the holidays, retelling the best story ever told.

The First to Say . . .

BY TAMMY MARCELAIN

On December 24th, I answer my phone and shout "CHRISTMAS EVE GIFT." If it's not a family member, I apologize to the caller, explaining that my strange response is due to a game my family plays on Christmas Eve.

My paternal family celebrates a tradition that has lasted many generations. We play a game called, "Christmas Eve Gift." On the day before Christmas, any family member who talks to another family member, by phone or in person, will try to be the first to utter these three words: "Christmas Eve gift."

The words are not just said. They are screamed, blurted, screeched, whatever it takes to say them before the other is finished saying the three words. Each player races to the word "gift." The greeting is said as fast as it can be spoken, and even though victory is brief, whoever finishes first is the winner.

Everyone has developed their own strategies to win. Here are a few of mine. Several years ago, I used to answer any phone call with, "Christmas Eve gift." Caller ID now helps unsuspecting callers avoid the prize-winning words. But it seemed to make even the uninitiated merry when they phoned expecting a calm, "Hello," and instead got an exclaimed CHRISTMAS EVE GIFT!

Another tactic of mine is by far the most difficult, occurring when I talk on the phone with family grouped in another's home. Sneaky, they hand the phone to another family member. When the conversation is over with one person, I don't know when the next person will begin to speak. So I repeat the three words over and over.

Sometimes I say them twenty times before the next cousin, aunt, or uncle gets to the phone. Or sometimes they've been there all along, just listening to hear me make a fool of myself.

My conniving brother Will often waits silently until I take a breath, acting like he's just picked up the receiver, and then he shouts the words in the midst of my gasping for air. Out of my siblings, Will is the distinct "Christmas Eve gift" champ.

The real gift is the fun my family experiences. Inevitable giggles follow the three words. The three words trigger smiles. The momentary satisfaction of winning brings a huge rush. It's also gratifying to hear an opponent say, "Oh, that was so close," or "I almost had it." Even a loser's groans are music to the winner's ears.

The losers in my family have learned to put bold holiday energy into a really good groan and cause everyone to laugh again. This game brings my family far and wide together—united even if it is only on the phone. We keep this tradition alive by playing the game from state-to-state, and in the past, country-to-country, or most often just down the street.

My tweener children enjoy the tradition, too. Guests are warned beforehand about the multiple family greeting they'll receive. The giggly-game heralds the gift of togetherness, in a room, across miles, and across the years.

Wish me luck. If you phone my home on December 24th, don't be surprised if you hear a special recorded message, because I want to be the first to say, "Christmas Eve gift."

It's my new strategy.

MORNING STAR LIGHT

I will see you again and you
will rejoice, and no one will
take away your joy.

JOHN 16:22

WORD QUILTERS' WISDOM

Despite circumstances,
choose joy.

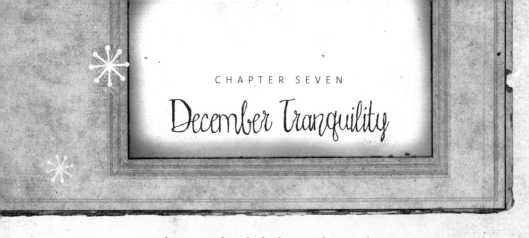

December Tranquility

*Glory to God in the highest, and on earth peace
to men on whom his favor rests.* LUKE 2:14

A LONG WINTER NAP, A COZY FIREPLACE, TIME TO READ THE GOSPEL
OF LUKE, A SOOTHING CUP OF CHAMOMILE TEA, A QUIET EVENING WITH
FRIENDS—SIMPLE PLEASURES CAN BRING HARMONY TO THIS BUSY MONTH.

FAMILY SNAPSHOT

Grandma's Snow Angel

BY KAREN ROBBINS

The snow lay perfectly on the ground, not too wet, not too dry. It sparkled as the rays of the sun danced over the crisp flakes. Too tempting. She struggled into her winter parka, pulled her hood up, and wound a scarf around her neck. A smile lit her face as she tucked her feet into her boots, pulled on her gloves, and walked out the door.

The snow invited her with its freshness, only a few feet from the little landing in front of her condominium. She stepped into the unspoiled whiteness and turned.

Could she risk falling backward? Would it cushion her fall? Her sharp eye judged the depth and softness. Sure. She could do it.

Back she fell, arms outstretched into the pillowed white that covered the ground. She landed with a little grunt. Arms and legs still intact, she swished them back and forth. Yes. Now if she could just get up without ruining the image, there would be a perfect imprint of an angel in the snow. With eyes closed, she lay still for a moment— savoring the feeling of her accomplishment. She drank in the cold crisp air and relished the feel of the little flakes that still fell and melted against her cheeks.

Time to get up. She contemplated the best course of action.

"Everything okay, Snip?" a man's voice boomed. Startled, her eyes popped open and she saw her neighbor standing over her, concern written across his face.

She laughed. "I'm fine . . . if you'll give me a hand up, you'll help me preserve what I've made here."

He extended his hand and she delicately removed herself from the image in the snow. She noticed his puzzled expression.

"It's a snow angel," she explained, beginning to feel a bit embarrassed. After all, what was a seventy-nine-year-old great-grandmother doing outside making angels in the snow?

"Oh, yes, I see it now," he exclaimed. He seemed a little embarrassed too, having misunderstood her predicament.

"Thanks for the hand up," she told him. She wanted to ease his discomfort. "I didn't know how I was going to get up without ruining a perfectly good snow angel."

"It is a good snow angel," he said. "Glad I could help out." She saw him shake his head as he returned to his condo.

"It was a good snow angel," she repeated when she finished relating her story to us. "One of the best I've made."

My mother-in-law is one in a million. She raised five wonderful children while holding down a full-time job all those years. When she retired at age 62 at the Department of Health, she took up downhill skiing and learned to play golf. I think my father-in-law lived vicariously through her activities. He preferred less physically demanding hobbies such as restoring old cars.

Very little has slowed her down in the years since retirement. A bout with painful shingles kept her activities limited for a while. Then my father-in-law's diabetes led to a time when her attention was solely directed at his care.

We worried when he died—that her enthusiasm for life might drain. We shouldn't have. While she misses him dearly, she is a lady full of life and appreciative of all it has to offer—proved by that first senior snow angel.

She is now 86. Just before her birthday, there was one last snowfall—one last opportunity before the springtime would burst through and bring the pleasures of blossoming flowers and warm sunshine. As we walked to her door, there in the little patch of yard in front of the condo was a perfect snow angel.

We took a picture for unbelievers, for us—a reminder that life is what you make of it. If we look for ways to overcome the challenges life brings, we can all make "angels in the snow."

BETHLEHEM STAR

And the peace of God, which transcends all understanding,
will guard your hearts and your minds in Christ Jesus.

PHILIPPIANS 4:7

GINGERBREAD GENEALOGY

Christmas Carols ~ TERRA HANGEN

The first carol is recorded in the Bible, when angels appeared in the sky above the shepherds on the night of Jesus' birth. "Suddenly a great company of the heavenly host appeared with the angel, praising God and saying, 'Glory to God in the highest, and on earth peace to men on whom his favor rests'" (Luke 2:13-14). To pinpoint the first carol sung by people rather than angels is difficult.

The classic "Silent Night" is a favorite of many. On December 24, 1818, Joseph Mohr, priest at St. Nicholas Church in Oberndorf, Austria, faced the challenge of a rusted church organ, rendering it not usable. The priest needed music for the Christmas Eve services that didn't require organ accompaniment, and quickly set his poem "*Stille Nacht, Heilige Nacht*" to music. Franz Gruber, local organist, and Mohr sang "Silent Night" in church that evening, accompanied by guitar.

From this simple beginning, "Silent Night" spread across the region. In 1834, the traveling Strasser Family Singers sang it for King Frederick William IV of Prussia. The King so loved the carol he commanded it sung each Christmas Eve by his cathedral choir. The carol became popular around the world, translated into 300 languages and dialects.

"Hark the Herald Angels Sing" is another favorite of carolers, written by Charles Wesley and published in *Hymns and Sacred Poems* in 1739. The original opening line, "Hark! How all the welkin rings!" is no longer used. Welkin means "the vault of heaven overhead."

In the still of the night, when the welkin rings with joyful carols, we're reminded of those herald angels with celestial voices. The angel voices, so many years ago, that brought good tidings to Bethlehem shepherds.

VINTAGE POETRY

The time draws near the birth of Christ:
The moon is hid; the night is still;
The Christmas bells from hill to hill
Answer each other in the mist.

Four voices of four hamlets round,
From far and near, on mead and moor,
Swell out and fail, as if a door
Were shut between me and the sound:

Each voice four changes on the wind,
That now dilate, and now decrease,
Peace and goodwill, goodwill and peace,
Peace and goodwill, to all mankind.

VOICES IN THE MIST
BY ALFRED, LORD TENNYSON 1809-1892

A FEW OF OUR FAVORITE THINGS
Creative Gifts for Others

BRENDA

One Christmas, instead of mailing the usual Christmas cards, which are usually tossed away soon afterwards, we gave chocolate bars to family and friends with a holiday greeting on the wrapper. The cost equaled high-quality cards and postage. A program on my computer designs candy bar wrappers. I buy the large, 5-ounce dark chocolate bars when they're on sale for $1 and then print out a personalized wrapper—a chocolate bar with an individual wrap is special and appreciated.

CATHY

My daughter, Sheryle, gave me a small fancy box, inside were 30 slips of paper and inexpensive gifts—chocolate, travel-size lotion, a small candle. On the notes were instructions for relaxation. She told me to draw out one slip of paper each day and follow the advice. Her suggestions: drink hot tea on your porch; phone a "long-distance" friend, read for 30 minutes, drink coffee from your favorite tea cup, take a bubble bath, and go for a stroll—not for exercise—but to enjoy nature. She said, "If one activity doesn't fit your schedule, put it back and draw another." These ordained Sabbath moments helped me stop, relax, and refocus. Give a similar gift to a busy friend.

KAREN

For our pastor's family, I prepared meatloaf and froze it. In a large decorated basket, I placed meatloaf, a bag of frozen veggies, frozen mashed potatoes, and homemade cookies. I delivered it at the onset of the holidays, and they stashed the minute-meal in their freezer until needed on a busy night.

LESLIE

Our favorite quickie gift is the Movie Lover's Pack. We hot glue a package of microwave popcorn and a box of Junior Mints or any special "movie theater candy" together, and add a $5.00 gift certificate to a local video store. We keep several on hand for pop-ins bearing gifts. We also give these to service providers—letter and newspaper carriers, hair stylists, etc.

TERRA

For the gardeners on your list, gift a subscription to "Green Prints: The Weeder's Digest." Articles range from the dark "Squirrel Wars" to "Love and Daffodils Forever." One year, 4 issue subscription. www.greenprints.com

TRISH

Consider helping with repairs at a local Christian camp site during Christmas break. I feel it's important for our children to participate in giving back. We spend a few days every October at Camp Luther Work Weekend, cleaning and painting. Our family of six spends a week there every summer as campers, but now that the kids are old enough, we help shut the camp for the winter.

A GIFT FOR YOU

Silent Night ~ Cathy Messecar

To help your family during this busy month, give them the gift of silence. In your home, designate a quiet hour each evening, a time when no outside influence is allowed through any cable or wireless receivers. That means turning off the TV, radio, computer, electronic games, landlines, and cell phones. In this blessed season, allow your family to experience "all is calm" in the silent-night hour.

Helen Steiner Rice's poem, "The Story of the Christmas Guest" is about Conrad, a shopkeeper, whom the Lord told in a dream that he would visit on Christmas Day. Three times that day, persons arrived at Conrad's door needing help—a shabby beggar, an elderly woman, and a lost child. Each time Conrad assisted his unexpected guests, but at nightfall, disappointment filled his heart because he hadn't seen the Lord. The Lord let Conrad know that when he helped the visitors at his door he'd met and helped the Lord.

Helen Steiner Rice Foundation claims no copyright to the story because Helen heard the story from her grandmother Beiri. Leo Tolstoy wrote a similar short story about a shoemaker, "Where Love Is, God Is," based on a French folktale. The originator of the beloved storyline is difficult to identify. In recent years and based on similar folklore, Reuben Salliens, Mig Holder, and Julie Downing collaborated on an illustrated children's book, *Papa Panov's Special Day.*

"The Story of the Christmas Guest" is often presented in Christmas pageants and recitals, and has been recorded by many musicians over the years: Grandpa Jones, Andy Griffith, Johnny Cash, the Ricky Skaggs Family, and Reba McEntire.

PEPPERMINTS FOR LITTLE ONES

Handmade Cards ~ CATHY MESSECAR

Assist children in making Christmas greeting cards and thank you cards.
Furnish paper, stick-glue, crayons, envelopes, and safety scissors. After little
ones assemble their masterpieces, help them hand deliver one or two greeting
cards before Christmas to shut-ins. After the holidays, assist them in
addressing and mailing thank you cards for gifts received.

COOKIE CANISTER

Mary's Oatmeal Cookies ~ CATHY MESSECAR

This recipe passed from Mary to Irene to Joyce to Doris to Cathy and on to you and makes the best oatmeal cookie I've tasted.

Triple sift:
1 ½ cups flour, ½ tsp. salt, 1 tsp. baking powder, and 1 tsp. baking soda.
Cream: 2 cups brown sugar, 1 cup shortening, 2 eggs, and 1 tsp. vanilla. Add dry ingredients. Add 3 cups rolled oats and 1 cup chopped nuts. Chill dough. Shape into walnut-size balls. Roll in confectioner's sugar before baking. Grease cookie sheet and bake 2 – 3 inches apart at 375° for 8 minutes. Do not over bake. Yield: 5-6 dozen

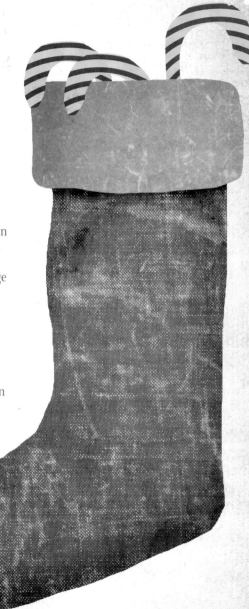

STOCKING STUFFER TRADITION

Santa's Chair ~ CATHY MESSECAR

At the beginning of December, designate a chair in
a quiet corner of your house as the "Santa Chair."
Place a comfy afghan, throw pillow, or even a huge
red bow on the chair back. Anytime someone
in the family needs a break from conversation,
household noises, or the hoopla, they can retire
to the chair for a few quiet moments. Yes, moms
and grandmas, this can be a ten-minute relaxation
chair for you—a time out to recover from the
Christmas bustle, too.

EVERGREEN THUMB

Cyclamen ~ Terra Hangen

Cyclamen is a small plant admired for its Christmas-time flowers, which glow in brilliant fuchsia, purple, pink, and holiday red and white. Native to the Holy Lands, it is believed to be one of the flowers Jesus described when he said, "Consider how the lilies grow. They do not labor or spin. Yet I tell you, not even Solomon in all his splendor was dressed like one of these" (Luke 12:27).

The Cyclamen sold by florists and nurseries resembles the Cyclamen growing wild in Galilee. Cyclamen persicum decora with its deep pink flowers is a cultivated version of the Holy Land flower. Popular in American gardens for naturalizing is the white or lavender flowered Cyclamen coum, and Cyclamen neopolitan, with pink or white flowers. Most Cyclamen flourish in garden zones 5–9.

For indoor plants at Christmas, provide bright light, but not direct hot sun. A plant may be watered near the rim of the pot, but do not splash the leaves. The best watering method is to place the pot in a saucer of water for twenty minutes. Next, set the pot in a saucer filled with pebbles and water. This provides humidity, but make sure the pebbles lift the pot above the water to avoid "wet feet" which can damage your plant. A blooming Cyclamen is a welcome holiday gift that brightens any room.

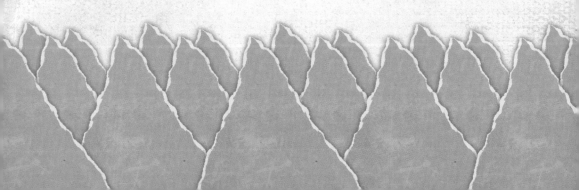

Let It Snow

by D'Ann Mateer

As my husband and I braved the bitter cold and made our way into the eleven o'clock Christmas Eve service at church, we imagined the disappointment that would cloud our children's faces the next morning. A few flurries, a veritable powdered sugar dusting of the world, would not fulfill their eager longings to experience their first real snow. An hour later, picking our way through the parking lot, careful not to slip, we again lamented that we could do nothing to produce the results they desired.

For several years, our children looked forward to a Christmas in their father's Pennsylvania hometown, dreaming of that elusive white Christmas that only appears in songs in Dallas, Texas. We'd arrived in the state, only to find remnants of dirty snow around the edges of brown yards. The wind blew bitter cold, but no new snow fell.

From the Christmas Eve service, we made our way back to the house, careful not to wake the sleeping children in the back seat of the car, careful not to burst their visions of snow-covered sugarplums. The morning would come soon enough for them to understand what we had told them: even in the mountains of central Pennsylvania, Christmas snow is rare.

But God gave us a Christmas gift that night—the gift of snow. Not just a dusting—a deluge. Six inches fell in a few short hours. My starry-eyed Southern children awoke to a world transformed into marshmallow white. Their first white Christmas. Their first real snow.

In borrowed boots and flimsy knit mittens, they tromped into the frozen world. I sat cozy in the house, sipping coffee, watching through the window as my children built their first snowman with their dad, Uncle Jeff, and Pappy. The stockings still bulged with goodies. The packages remained unopened under the tree. The best Christmas surprises on that morning—snowmen, sled rides, and snowball fights.

Only after faces turned red, fingers went numb, and blue jeans hung wet and cold against their legs did the normal business of Christmas commence. After steaming mugs of hot chocolate and changes of clothes, they opened long-awaited presents, but their eyes strayed to the windows again.

Fresh, dry, warm clothes were destined for cold and wet.

I don't remember the presents we received that year, and my children don't either. Instead, we remember the first time they saw Pappy's yard custom-blanketed in white. We marvel at the faithfulness of the One who sent the baby in the manger, the One who answered the prayer of my children's hearts. He let it snow, let it snow, let it snow.

MORNING STAR LIGHT

Jesus said to his disciples,
"Come with me by yourselves to a quiet
place and get some rest."

MARK 6:31

WORD QUILTERS' WISDOM

Instead of purchasing extra holiday glitz,
seek serenity.

CHAPTER EIGHT

Rejoice Little Child

*On coming to the house, they saw the child with his mother Mary,
and they bowed down and worshiped him.* MATTHEW 2:11

A CHILD'S BRIGHT EYES AND CONTAGIOUS JOY ADD SPARKLE TO THE HOLIDAYS. YOUNG LAUGHTER

REFRESHES. RECAPTURE A SENSE OF WONDER FROM THE HAPPY, LAVISH SENTIMENTS OF CHILDREN.

FAMILY SNAPSHOT

Picture Perfect

BY LESLIE WILSON

Portrait Day loomed. My parents took advantage of having family members in town for the holidays, creating a photo op of magnanimous proportions.

Mom wanted us color-coordinated—red and black with a touch of plaid. And blue jeans thrown in for my husband. I worried about what my children—Charlie, Molly, Reese, ages 6, 3, 2—should wear. I stressed over Molly's hair. Bow or no bow?

Portrait Day arrived. Though Christmas Eve and Day had depleted my energy, I had to motivate my team. "Hey, guys! It's picture day! Who wants to have a real photographer take their picture at Mimi and Granddad's house?"

My words floated away as if carried by the winter wind, the kids too enthralled with their toys from Santa. Tossing various outfits into a rolling suitcase, I hollered, "Who wants to go to Granddad's house for hot cakes and bacon?" Instant cooperation.

When we arrived, everyone else—including my 96-year-old grandmother—was already there and dressed.

"Why aren't the kids ready?" someone asked. Gee, I wish I'd thought of that. I smiled, and then recounted a few highlights of my morning. That's when my mom, my husband Bret, and I played man-to-man defense, each taking a kid to get them ready. A battle ensued.

Charlie, age 6, wired from too much sugar, not enough sleep, and enough toys to equip an orphanage, giggled and wiggled, but eventually cooperated.

Molly, age 3, didn't want to put on "da dwess, Mommy." She wailed and squirmed, as I poked one arm, then the other through pooffy sleeves. I smoothed the plaid skirt into place. Now, the hair. I smiled at my unsuspecting daughter.

We wrestled.

I tugged.

She bawled. Loudly.

Through screams, I combed her hair into the previously chosen style. I won—sort of. Her hair remained styled, but she wouldn't let go of her tantrum. I enticed her with treats, hugs, and new toys. She pooh-poohed all, content with torturing her perfectionist mother.

Reese, age 2, took on my mom. Once, he escaped her grasp, streaking through the living room wearing only his tighty-whities. Mom chased after him, scooping him into her arms. "Oh, no you don't, you little stinker. You can't wear undies for a family picture. Mimi has a special, new outfit just for Reeser." Her strategy worked, and he relaxed in her arms.

The photographer arrived. He set up reflectors, checked the lighting, and announced, "Showtime."

We weren't ready. Anger in the form of "You had better shape up this instant, Missy!" hadn't worked to calm Molly's fit. Neither had bribery. I carried her outside. The wintry December air took our breaths away—which made Molly stop crying. She popped her thumb into her mouth—her classic comforting move.

"Punkin' Girl, Mimi and Granddad just want to get a nice picture of the whole family. Uncle Brian and Aunt Claudia don't come to Texas very often. Nana's getting old. This may be the last time we can take a special picture with everyone in it. And you look so beautiful in your Christmas dress! Can you calm down and smile pretty for Mommy . . . please?"

After a pause, she nodded her head, never removing her thumb from her mouth.

Mission accomplished.

With the photo ordeal over, my dad asked, "Les, would you like to have a picture of your immediate family?"

"Sure, Dad. That would be great," I heard my mouth say. My mind asked, Haven't we been through enough?

Bret and I sat in front of the fireplace, while Mom arranged children around us. Reese wouldn't sit still. He hopped up to look at remaining presents under the tree.

"No, Big Guy," my dad said pulling Reese away from the tree and its bounty. "Those presents are for some of Granddad's out-of-town relatives. We have to leave those wrapped."

He jumped up again to grab a Christmas cookie.

He scooted away to ring the front door bell. "Deck the Halls" rang out. With each escape, Mom or Dad—sometimes both—carried him back to his spot.

Charlie cracked jokes—sharing groaners from a book he'd opened the day before.

Molly, uncharacteristically still, refused to take her thumb out of her mouth.

Candy! It occurred to me that if she sucked on candy, she couldn't also be sucking her thumb. Mimi brought an enormous piece of fudge. Molly popped in the whole thing, grinning at me through chocolate teeth.

The photographer began snapping photo after photo—many of them during Reese's return visits to Bret's lap.

I smiled. I had won—or had I?

Two weeks later Mom and I looked through the proofs. The extended family shots turned out surprisingly well. Molly smiled in none of them—totally out of character for her happy, never-met-a-stranger personality.

Then we turned to our Wilson family photos. Proof after proof told the same story.

Charlie, my jokester, had stuck his thumb and forefinger in the nostrils of a bronze bust of a horse—in every picture. Hadn't the photographer seen him? But none of my other family members had said anything either. And they had all watched the debacle—drawn to it like a bad wreck on the highway. I reasoned they overlooked Charlie because Molly and Reese had stolen the show—as if they'd been the squeaky wheel shouting, "Hey, grease over here!"

Molly's nose showed up Rudolph-red from crying and blowing it dozens of times. She also had a wad in her cheek, not tobacco as future generations might speculate, but fudge. None showed wiggly Reese completely in focus. We eventually chose one with a clear shot of his face. I resolved not to dwell on his blurry legs and feet.

My frustration burned. Why couldn't my kids understand the importance of a family portrait? For a grand total of five minutes, why couldn't they have stayed still, smiled pretty, and kept hands in laps? Why couldn't I have controlled the situation better to create the outcome I wanted—a perfect family picture?

Flash forward six years. A freelance writer sits at her desk, desperate for inspiration. She spies the corner of a picture frame and pulls the photo from its hiding place behind a row of standing files. In this first family photo, boasting color-coordinated outfits, in front of a roaring fireplace, the parents' smiles seem forced, as if plastered on in their determination to make the best of a bad situation. The oldest son grins devilishly, his digits inserted into the nostrils of a bronze horse head. Offsetting the daughter's frown is a decidedly pink nose and an enormous bulge in one cheek. The youngest boy is half-blur.

Staring at what could have been our finest hour, I finally get it.

I wanted this family picture—one that would capture the essence, not just the physical appearance, of my children at ages 6, 3 and 2. And that's exactly what I got.

I only wish it hadn't taken me so long to figure it out.

BETHLEHEM STAR

God, your God, has set you above your companions
by anointing you with the oil of joy.

HEBREWS 1:9

GINGERBREAD GENEALOGY

Christmas Stockings ~ CATHY MESSECAR

The Christmas stocking is hung near the hearth on Christmas Eve with hope that Santa Claus will fill it with candy, fruit, and nuts. Some believe the tradition of holiday stockings came from Germany where children hung an everyday sock on their bedposts on Christmas Eve. Others think the Dutch tradition preceded Christmas stockings: children left clogs, filled with hay, by the hearth for St. Nicholas' reindeer.

The most prominent legend says a nobleman fell on hard times and had no money for his daughters' dowries, leaving the three with no hope of marrying. One evening St. Nicholas passed by and saw the daughters hanging their fresh-washed stockings to dry by the fireplace. Knowing their predicament, St. Nicholas tossed gold coins down the chimney and they landed in the maidens' stockings. Imagine their surprise and relief when the secret gift changed their fate.

Buy gold-wrapped chocolate "coins" for children's stockings and retell this legend

VINTAGE LYRICS

Lully, lullay, Thou little tiny Child,
By, by, lully, lullay.
O sisters too, how may we do,
For to preserve this day
This poor Youngling for Whom we sing
By, by, lully, lullay?
Herod the king, in his raging,

Charged he hath this day
His men of might, in his own sight,
All young children to slay.
That woe is me, poor Child for Thee!
And ever morn' and day
For Thy parting neither say nor sing,
By, by, lully, lullay.

LYRICIST UNKNOWN

STOCKING STUFFER TRADITION

Recycled Reading ~ TRISH BERG

After Thanksgiving, we round up our Christmas books into one big pile. Then I secretly wrap them and place them under the tree. Each night, one child picks a book to unwrap and we read that as our bedtime story. Every year I surprise them and buy several new books and also mix in a few library books. It's an inexpensive and unique way to get them excited about reading and Christmas.

A FEW OF OUR FAVORITE THINGS
Children's Books

BRENDA

Does God Know How to Tie Shoes? by Nancy White Carlstrom

You Are Special, Max Lucado

CATHY

Pokey Little Puppy's First Christmas, a Little Golden Book

Christmas Lizard by Cory Edwards

KAREN

The Littlest Angel by Charles Tazewell

LESLIE

The Little House on the Prairie series by Laura Ingalls Wilder, especially the
Christmas chapters. On vacation, riding and reading aloud to the family,
my voice faltered and my right side went numb, signaling a stroke. Now
fully recovered, the series holds a special place in my family's hearts.

TERRA

Little Drummer Boy by Ezra Jack Keats. The same paperback edition
we bought many years ago is still for sale for only $6.99. What a bargain.

TRISH

The Crippled Lamb by Max Lucado

"The Coventry Carol" melody and beginning lyrics "Lully, lullay, Thou little tiny Child, By, by, lully, lullay" are most likely familiar. Even though performed at Christmastime, the song doesn't tell of Jesus' wondrous birth. The mournful tune is about Herod's edict to slaughter the innocent young boys of Bethlehem, "[Herod] gave orders to kill all the boys in Bethlehem who were two years old and under" (Matthew 2:16). Warned in a dream, Joseph, the earth-father of Jesus, secreted his family away by night.

The Shearmen and Tailor guilds performed this song in Coventry, England, in the fifteenth century. On rolling pageant wagons, the guilds performed their written plays, often themed around the birth, death, and resurrection of Jesus Christ. In the play about King Herod's atrocious decree, actor-mothers sang this lullaby to quiet their babes in hopes that the king's soldiers wouldn't hear even a whimper.

On December 28th, some celebrate The Feast of the Holy Innocents. Since the sixth century, this feast has commemorated the babes in Bethlehem, considered the first martyrs for the cause of Christ. "The Coventry Carol" is the most haunting of all Christmas carols because it portrays the need of fallen man for a Savior who will save us from ourselves. Carefully listen to the lyrics next time you hear, "Lully, Lullay," meaning, "I saw, I saw." If we really see our need for the Christ Child, we can rejoice in his coming.

PEPPERMINTS FOR LITTLE ONES

Better to Give ~ LESLIE WILSON

Wrap a present for Jesus, leaving an opening in the top. Write your gifts to him on a slip of paper and drop it into the box. On Christmas morning, open His gift, and share with each other what you gave to Jesus.

A GIFT FOR YOU

Taste Bud Teaser ~ BRENDA NIXON

To fill your kitchen with a light aroma of home baked cookies, simply put a teaspoon of vanilla extract on a small square of aluminum foil, corners folded up, and place in a warm oven. The heat releases the fragrance and tickles the taste buds.

EVERGREEN THUMB

Holly ~ TERRA HANGEN

Holly branches provide festive Christmas decorations and symbolize devotion and constancy. For an ongoing Christmas tradition, buy a small holly bush in a decorative pot, display it indoors at Christmas, and plant it outside in spring.

One Christmas my dad and stepmother sent us a pretty holly plant, which graced our table for the holidays. In April, we planted it outside, anticipating many years of holly boughs at Christmastime.

For most hollies, only the female plant provides berries, with flowers in late spring to early summer and red berries from autumn to March. Birds—robins, cedar waxwings, cardinals, and goldfinches—flock to the crimson berries. To optimize berry production, plant a female and a male holly in a sunny spot.

Red Beauty and Satyr Hill are excellent garden hollies. The finest fruiting holly is Old Heavy Berry, which grows 30 to 40 feet tall, and has masses of brick-red pea-sized berries.

COOKIE CANISTER

Yummy Squares ~ CATHY MESSECAR

This recipe passed from my mother-in-law, Nancy, to me. They are very light, scrumptious bars. The frothy egg white, brown sugar, and pecan top layer is a delicate praline-like topping.

½ cup shortening	½ tsp. salt	½ cup chopped pecans
1 cup sugar	1 tsp. baking powder	1 ½ cups flour
2 eggs (well beaten)	1 egg white	1 cup brown sugar
		1 tsp. vanilla

Cream shortening and sugar, add eggs and vanilla, and then add dry ingredients. Mix well. Grease and flour a 13 x 9 x 2 glass dish. Spread batter in pan. Beat egg white until moist soft peaks form. Add brown sugar to egg whites and fold in nuts. Spread over batter. Bake at 375° for 25 minutes until golden brown on top. Cut into squares. Sprinkle with confectioner's sugar. For moist, chewy consistency, store in airtight container.

The First Christmas Without Santa

BY JUDY BOWYER

"**M**ama!" I yelled as the back screen door banged shut behind me. Mama hated slamming doors, but I'd walked all through the house to find her. I had important information.

"Guess what? I learned to spell 'Tip' today—P-I-T!" My first day of first grade and I'd already blown it. Mama just smiled, handing me the clothes she unclipped from the clothesline. My chattering continued. "Know what else? Peggy said there's no Santa Claus." I complained. "I told her she was wrong." Mama made no comment.

Later, while I set the table for supper, I asked, "Mama, is there a Santa Claus?" I held my breath for the answer.

As Mama stirred a pot on the stove, she "answered" with a single question, "What do you think?"

"Well, I always get presents under the tree. Somebody has to bring them."

Although reasonably sure Santa Claus existed, a problematic question lingered. I knew how long it took just to drive to Lubbock to buy school clothes. So, how could Santa travel all over the world in just one night?

Maybe I should quiz my most trusted sources about the existence of Santa Claus. Later, I asked my older sister—she knew everything.

"Sometimes you can be so stupid!" she huffed. Not exactly a clear answer.

I asked my cousin Sheri. Although a bit younger, she seemed wise to me. She threw back her head and giggled—her trademark reaction, and said, "Of course not! Don't you know anything?"

Connie, the Methodist preacher's daughter, lived next door. Wouldn't she know the truth? But as we sat crouched in the sandbox behind my house, she admitted, "I don't know for sure, but I don't think Santa is real. I think it's your mom and dad."

Horrified, I started to protest, but she continued conspiratorially. "The thing is, if they know you don't believe in Santa anymore, you'll stop getting presents." That new piece of information threw an entirely different light on the dilemma.

That fall, I learned to read in Miss Hassie Taylor's first grade class. The *Jack and Janet, Tip and Mitten* readers expanded my horizons. My knowledge grew, and I even learned to spell T-I-P, but the Santa Claus mystery never strayed far from my mind.

Christmas approached, bringing its usual preparations. We chose a fragrant tree and positioned it, as always, in front of the picture window in our living room. Wrapped packages mysteriously appeared underneath the tree. Mama decorated Christmas cookies. I painstakingly printed my letter to Santa on a page from my Big Chief tablet. My aunt, who worked at the post office, assured my letter special delivery to the North Pole. Expectations mounted as school dismissed for the holidays and town folk buzzed about the possibility of snow.

On the night of December 23rd, unable to sleep, I crept out of bed and tiptoed down the hall. The lights from the Christmas tree still shone in the darkened living room. I stood, watching the bubble lights on the tree, and suddenly my dad appeared.

"Whatcha doin'?" he said softly.

"I can't sleep, Daddy."

"Come here," he said, sitting in the rocker next to the tree. I crawled onto his lap. As we rocked, I snuggled up next to his chest to keep warm.

Neither of us spoke for several minutes, but troubled in spirit, I finally whispered, "Daddy, I don't know what to do about Santa Claus."

I cannot remember my dad's exact words. I do remember his soothing, gentle voice, his big hands holding me close. Because of his obvious love, I felt safe, respected and relieved when he told me the truth. I felt great peace that night.

In spite of Connie's dire warning, Santa continued to leave gifts under our Christmas tree. The difference—I realized that a remote man from far away didn't deliver them. Instead of a stranger, the gifts now represented loving parents, who didn't have much money but understood their little girl's heart.

I quit believing in Santa Claus that year, but I gained something far more precious—a picture of God's always-love. From my daddy, I learned how God wants us to crawl into his lap for intimate conversations, and how much He wants to tell us the truth and give us good things.

What a spectacular trade-off.

MORNING STAR LIGHT

But Jesus called the children to him
and said, "Let the little children come to me,
and do not hinder them, for the kingdom of
God belongs to such as these."

LUKE 18:16

WORD QUILTERS' WISDOM

A child's joy is contagious.
Catch some.

CHAPTER NINE

"Mary" Memories

Mary treasured up all these things and pondered them in her heart. LUKE 2:19

A MOTHER'S SCRAPBOOK HOLDS PHOTOS, PRIZE RIBBONS, AND STICK

FIGURE DRAWINGS. LOCKED INSIDE A MOTHER'S HEART—INTANGIBLE

SMILES, HOPES, UNDYING LOVE, AND PRAYERS FOR HER CHILDREN.

FAMILY SNAPSHOT

A Purple Stocking

BY KAREN ROBBINS

I'm a traditionalist. I decorate with the basic Christmas colors—green and red. At least I did before my mother asked my adopted six-year-old daughter, "Cheryl, what color stocking would you like me to make for you?"

My mother had knitted red and green stockings for our three older boys. Now that we had adopted Cheryl and her five-year-old brother, Don, my mother was eager to begin theirs.

Cheryl made her choice loud and clear, "Purple!"

"Purple it is," my mother said, her raised brows thwarting my impending protest. I knew the stocking's importance to Cheryl for this time Santa might actually fill it.

In the past, Cheryl hung stockings but Santa never put anything into them. The most Cheryl and Don ever received was a truck and a doll from social services, usually a few days after Christmas. The magic of Christmas Eve eluded them.

Anticipation and anxiety rose as Christmas neared. My twelve-year-old twins, Rob and Ron, and nine-year-old Andy could not comprehend that Cheryl and Don had never experienced the frenzied moments of sheer joy on Christmas morning, tearing through layers of wrappings and boxes.

Because Christmas fell on a Sunday, we changed our calendar and made Christmas Morning the 24th instead. That enabled me to plan a surprise visit from our neighborhood Santa on our Christmas Eve. That night, when Santa rang the doorbell, Cheryl flew to open it.

"Ho, ho, ho. So here you are." In mock surprise, Santa lifted his arms. "I've been looking for you. You and Donny moved so much that I found it hard to track you down. But now you have a forever home, so I know where you'll be."

"My stocking . . . purple stocking . . . hanging on fireplace." Cheryl, the chatterbox, was tongue-tied.

"Well, it's early to bed so I can bring Rudolph and the gang to fill that purple stocking." Santa chuckled.

"You're not landing on my roof are you, Santa?" my husband chided.

"Well, of course. Got to use the chimney. It's tradition, you know."

"Who's going to clean up that mess the reindeer leave?" Bob folded his arms across his chest. "I'm not."

"I will! I will!" Cheryl shouted, panic stricken that Santa might change his mind. Reassuring Cheryl of his return, Santa ho-ho-hoed and left.

Cheryl and Don were the first tucked into bed that night. Andy followed quickly. The sooner to bed—the sooner morning would come.

Rob and Ron held out to the last. They watched us begin "Santa's" traditional tree decorating, but to avoid total disillusionment, they went to bed before Bob and I finished.

Our Christmas Morning arrived with the sunrise. When we entered the family room, we found all five children sitting side by side, the tree lights on, staring at the stockings, heavy with goodies, now lined up at the base of the fireplace. They had dutifully waited for Mom and Dad to come down for breakfast.

"He did come! He did!" Cheryl exclaimed when we appeared in the doorway. She jumped up and down and pointed to her purple stocking.

"So he did," I said. The same excitement I remembered as a child filled me. "Well, look into your stockings, and then we'll have breakfast before we open the big gifts."

Cheryl cradled the purple stocking in her arms and joined the circle of siblings discovering the little candies, novelties, and fruit stuffed into their knitted stockings.

After breakfast, Bob poured his traditional second cup of coffee to heighten the anticipation, but the kids nudged him into the family room before the final sip.

We took turns opening gifts one at a time. Bob and I watched each expression. After a few rounds, I noticed the older boys had laid aside their opened gifts. Instead, they sat quietly, intrigued with their new brother and sister. Ron brushed a tear from his cheek. His face reddened as he turned to me.

"This really is the first Christmas for them, isn't it?"

I nodded and smiled.

The rest of the day was anything but traditional. Gift giving over, we gave our full attention to the Christmas Eve service which became more meaningful—the celebration of Christ's birth more joyous. That Christmas morning welcomed Cheryl and Don into our family as surely as God welcomes us through Jesus, his son.

The purple stocking hangs between the red and green ones each year. After all, purple is traditionally a royal color and Christmas celebrates the birth of the King.

BETHLEHEM STAR

And Jesus grew in wisdom and stature,
and favor with God and men.

LUKE 2:52

GINGERBREAD GENEALOGY

Luminaries ~ CATHY MESSECAR

Folks in the Southwest place luminaries along footpaths to light the way to churches or homes during holiday celebrations. Inexpensive construction begins with small brown paper bags with sand in the bottom, and a votive candle set in the sand. The custom came from Spain when, on Christmas Eve, monks lit crisscrossed sticks alongside trails to churches, pointing the way for worshipers.

VINTAGE POETRY

In the air made sweet by the breath of kine,
The little child in the manger lay,
The child, that would be king one day
Of a kingdom not human, but divine.

His mother Mary of Nazareth
Sat watching beside his place of rest,
Watching the even flow of his breath,
For the joy of life and the terror of death
Were mingled together in her breast.

THREE KINGS
BY HENRY WADSWORTH LONGFELLOW
AN EXCERPT

STOCKING STUFFER TRADITION

Name that Ancestor ~ CATHY MESSECAR

Jean Compton from Texas invented a unique game
for her grandchildren. She gathered photographs
of ancestors and rolls of quarters before children
arrived for the holiday dinner and gift exchange. On
the big day, she seated children around her and, using
the photos like flash cards, she shared names and told
tidbits about their kin in the pictures. Then she went
through the photographs a second time, rewarding
children with a quarter for each right answer.

She plays the game each year. A banker, she
now rewards her teen grandchildren two dollar bills
for correct answers. She said, "My grandkids know
their family history and can identify all of their
ancestors." Just call her Grandma Jeanealogy.

A FEW OF OUR FAVORITE THINGS
Hot Beverages

BRENDA
Mint mocha coffee. I love to sip on this while listening to my favorite musical group, Il Divo.

CATHY
Wassail or even a cup of apple juice with cinnamon candies melting in the bottom of the cup.

KAREN
Chai Tea is soothing and restful during a busy day.

LESLIE
I like Celestial Seasoning's Sleepytime.

TERRA
Green tea with brown rice—Eden Organic Genmaicha Tea—the combination of green tea and roasted brown rice creates a lovely aroma.

TRISH
Peppermint hot cocoa: add a drop of peppermint flavoring to favorite hot chocolate and a small candy cane for a stirrer.

TRIVIA TREASURES

In forty minutes, Mel Torme turned thoughts of "Chestnuts roasting . . . Jack Frost nipping . . . Yuletide carols . . . Folks dressed up like Eskimos," into a Christmas classic, penned during a summer heat wave in 1945.

PEPPERMINTS FOR LITTLE ONES

Paper Chain ~ Cathy Messecar

In late November, cut 25 strips of bright colored construction paper 8 x 3 inches. On each write a simple activity you can do with your children during the month of December: make hot chocolate, eat popcorn, bake cookies, write a letter to Santa, play a board game, play charades using Christmas words, or help cook your favorite dinner. Form a chain from the strips of paper. Hang near the breakfast table, and then each morning let the children open one link. Some time that day, share in the suggested activity. This also gives children a visual countdown until Christmas Day.

Blue Christmas ~ CATHY MESSECAR

Many communities offer "Blue Christmas" services for the suffering. Memories of past sorrows or current troubles can especially bring on melancholy during the time when most everyone is rejoicing.

These services offer a time for reflection and renewal. If you need this quiet contemplation time, look for one where you live. Suggestions for organizing such an event are online. Gathering with folks who are also undergoing difficult times is uplifting. Comfort results from the reminder that "people living in darkness have seen a great light; on those living in the land of the shadow of death a light has dawned" (Matthew 4:16).

Chocolate Dipped Mocha Shortbread ~ CATHY MESSECAR

1 ½ cups flour
½ cup confectioner's sugar
½ cup plus 2 Tbs. butter (room temp)

½ tsp. vanilla
1 Tbs. instant coffee, ground into fine powder

Chocolate Dip: 8 oz. semi-sweet chocolate chips plus 1 Tbs. shortening

Place ingredients in bowl and combine thoroughly. Press into an 8 x 8 baking pan. Score into 16 squares, then score squares diagonally. Prick each triangle twice with fork. Bake at 325° until puffy and edges just start to brown. Cool in pan 5 min. Cut on scored lines. Cool completely. For chocolate coating, melt the chocolate chips and shortening in microwave on low setting. Dip one corner of triangle into chocolate. Let dry on cookie rack.

Petticoat Tails Shortbread: Leave out instant coffee and do not dip these in chocolate. Press into a round pie plate. Score into 16 wedges. Prick with fork. Follow directions above.

EVERGREEN THUMB

Rosemary Tree ~ Terra Hangen

Rosemary symbolizes remembrance, as William Shakespeare acknowledged in *Hamlet*: "There's rosemary, that's for remembrance; pray you love, remember." Mary is incorporated in this herb's name to symbolize Mary's faithfulness.

Representing faithfulness and remembrance, with its foliage resembling pine needles, Rosemary makes a lovely table top Christmas tree. You can buy a small Rosemary plant in spring and trim it to Christmas tree shape, or buy a ready-made Rosemary topiary Christmas tree in December.

Place your Rosemary Christmas tree near a sunny window, or buy two and place them on a front porch to greet visitors. Use lightweight tiny ornaments and ribbons to decorate this herb plant. Water when dry.

A sprig of Rosemary in your oven, with roasting pork, chicken or lamb will make your kitchen smell sensational and the meats will absorb the scent of Rosemary. Longer branches can be used to apply barbecue sauce to meats before or after grilling.

When the holiday ends, Rosemary thrives best outdoors in the ground or a container.

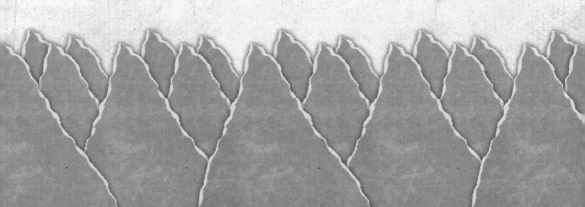

Little Angel Girl

BY TRISH BERG

She looks at me from her perch on the pine branch. Her eyes shine like the moon. Her skin is porcelain china, her wings feathery white. I call her my Little Angel Girl, and she reminds me of someone I loved and lost.

My Little Angel Girl is a Christmas ornament, given to me by my mother-in-law on the first Christmas after we lost our own baby daughter through a second trimester miscarriage. Each year when I gently position the ornament in the tree, I remember our little girl.

We had three beautiful children—Hannah, 6, Sydney, 4, and Colin nearly 2, when the home pregnancy kit showed a pink strip and I knew for sure a fourth child was due.

Months later, when my doctor asked if he could do an additional ultrasound to check on things, I didn't worry. He had said something about the likelihood of twins increasing with a mother's age. In my thirties now, that's what I thought he might be checking for—twins. That would be exhausting.

To my surprise, my doctor turned the ultrasound monitor out of view. I knew something must be wrong, and the look on his face made my heart pound. I gathered up my strength and asked, "What's wrong?"

He asked several questions. He then took my hand and told me that he could not find a heartbeat.

The tears flowed down my cheeks. A lump formed in my throat, like I'd swallowed a whole apple. He patted my back, and tried to reassure me with statistics of miscarriages and how I could try again.

I didn't want to try again. I wanted this baby.

He told me he would run more tests in a few days to make sure. He asked, "Is there anyone I can call to drive you home?"

I accepted more Kleenex and thanked him, "I think I want to drive myself home." I needed time alone. I wanted to sort through my feelings. I needed to cry without worrying about who might hear.

As I drove, I begged God to save this unborn child, to give me a miracle. But I knew in my heart that wouldn't happen. I felt His voice whisper to me, "I am enough for you. I will hold you."

The words held little comfort at the time. All I could think about was the little girl that I was powerless to save. I went through two weeks of tests before we had a final medical answer. God's most precious gift to me during that time was the assurance of a definitive answer.

That first Christmas after our loss was especially painful. Now, each Christmas when we decorate our tree, I place my Little Angel Girl ornament on a sturdy branch, right out front so I can see her radiant smile, because life is about loving those near and dear to us, even those we can only hold in our hearts.

MORNING STAR LIGHT

When Jesus saw his mother there, and the disciple whom he loved standing nearby, he said to his mother, "Dear woman, here is your son," and to the disciple, "Here is your mother." From that time on, [John] took her into his home.

JOHN 19:26-27

WORD QUILTERS' WISDOM

Life may bring us many mothers.
Express thanks to the women in your life.

CHAPTER TEN

Thanksgiving in December

The shepherds returned, glorifying and praising God for
all the things they had heard and seen. LUKE 2:20

NOT EVERY SWEATER WILL FIT. EVERY SWEET WILL NOT BE A FAVORITE. NOT EVERY

JINGLE WILL JANGLE AT THE RIGHT TIME. HOWEVER, GRATITUDE IS ALWAYS IN STYLE.

FAMILY SNAPSHOT

A New White Elephant Tradition

BY LESLIE WILSON

Party planners instructed our new Sunday school class to bring the "best" White Elephant they could find to our Christmas party.

Mine, a horrific plastic skull, perhaps designed to teach kids about the human head or as a gross Halloween decoration, solicited quite a reaction. The couple who opened it realized they had zero chance of anyone "stealing" their unpleasant gift. Others voiced relief that they had opted for a different package.

In the final round, a large, flat package remained. Before it could be opened, a couple stood and moved to the center of our large circle.

"Wait!" The man gently grasped the recipient's arm. "We want to share the story behind this gift before you open it."

We all listened with interest.

"No couple or family can keep this gift the entire year. Instead, try to pass it on as many times as possible. Then, whoever has it next Christmas must re-wrap it and bring it back to the White Elephant exchange. The tradition is to keep it going from house to house all year long."

"Tell them The Rule," his wife prodded.

"When you pass it on to someone else, you have to place it inside their home or place of business. You can't just leave it on their front porch."

The present—a life-size cardboard cutout of Elvis Presley!

Let the game begin.

Amid laughter and stories of White Elephants of Christmases past, the party continued. One young couple, who needed to get home to an infant, asked several folks to move their vehicles from blocking them. In an unselfish act, one guy offered to move the Suburban belonging to our fearless Sunday school teacher, Scott.

Bret and I stayed late to help tidy up. Once home, my parents, a.k.a. the baby-sitters, greeted us with big grins. After good-night hugs, Bret and I climbed the stairs to our room and our beckoning bed. I pulled back the king-sized quilt and screamed.

From the adjacent bathroom Bret shushed me—something about not waking up the kids—and hustled into our bedroom to see what caused the big fuss.

Staring at us, still partially covered by the quilt, was the cardboard cut-out of Elvis.

"What ... ? How ... ?" We sat on the bed, dumbfounded. Composure regained, we made a few phone calls to sort out the complicated mess.

Turned out, the fella at the party who moved Scott's Suburban slipped Elvis into the passenger seat. Scott didn't see The King until he actually opened his car door to leave. Not wanting to harbor "the fugitive" for long, he quickly hatched a plan.

My parents became accomplices to his diabolical plot. They allowed him to slip The King between our sheets, covering him with the quilt. I'm sure Scott chuckled all the way home.

We'd been "Punk'd." Scott had pulled one over on us. But, like Scott, we didn't hold onto Elvis for long. Bret and I formulated our own sinister strategy. It involved the law office of another close friend, Brad.

Bret nonchalantly—if conspicuously—carried Elvis under his arm to an upper floor at Lincoln Plaza in downtown Dallas. People stared as he fed the meter, squeezed through the revolving door, and waited for the elevator. Bret hoped the payoff would be worth any embarrassment.

He scoped out the law office—lunchtime. Office personnel were scarce. He inched down the hallway toward Brad's office and stopped as our friend's voice boomed out on a phone call. Bret "sat" the cardboard Elvis in the assistant's empty chair and left as stealthily as he had entered.

In the days following, Brad never mentioned the sudden appearance of an unwanted guest at his office. I couldn't stand the suspense and cornered him at church.

"Have you seen Elvis lately?"

"No," he said.

"Really?" I pressed. "He didn't suddenly appear . . . say, at your office last week?"

"No."

I was really steamed. How could I get him to admit it?

"So you're telling me you never saw Elvis in your office? Your assistant never saw him or mentioned anything about him?" Surely I had him now.

"No, I haven't seen Elvis at my office or anywhere else."

When I recounted my conversation and my frustration to Bret, he smiled. "Honey, you're putting way too much time and energy into this whole thing."

Then, Elvis resurfaced. To hear Michelle—the newest victim . . . er, recipient—tell the story, she'd completely undressed in her closet and screeched her best B-movie scream when she noticed Elvis staring at her from the shower.

Elvis didn't stay long. Another friend, Annette, borrowed several card tables from neighbors for a party. Michelle taped Elvis to the underside of her card table. Annette's husband Philip carried The King into their home, Trojan Horse-style.

That first Christmas with Elvis, we shared not only the cardboard cut-out of the aged King of Rock, but zany fun and grateful hearts for the friendships we held dear.

And I finally gained closure with Brad. Forgetting I was dealing with a lawyer, I had always referenced Elvis, whom Brad pointed out died in 1977. Therefore, he couldn't have seen Elvis in his office. My cross examination should have been: "Did you or any of your co-workers see a life-sized cardboard cut-out of Elvis Presley in or around the offices at Lincoln Plaza anytime during the month of January?"

Even that might not have worked.

Elvis could have already left the building.

BETHLEHEM STAR

Jesus then took the loaves, gave thanks, and distributed
to those who were seated as much as they wanted.

JOHN 6:11

GINGERBREAD GENEALOGY
Christmas Trees ~ LESLIE WILSON

For many, the Christmas tree is the hallmark of all holiday decorations. And though some mistakenly believe this symbol to be pagan in origin, Christmas trees derive their meaning from distinctly Christian roots.

Where did the notion that Christmas trees are pagan in origin come from? People occasionally misinterpret this scripture from Jeremiah 10:2-4: "This is what the Lord says . . . the customs of the peoples are worthless; they cut a tree out of the forest, and a craftsman shapes it with his chisel. They adorn it with silver and gold; they fasten it with hammer and nails so that it will not totter" (NIV).

Throughout Scripture, followers of God struggled with worshiping the created rather than the Creator. However, this passage from Jeremiah does not refer to cutting down and decorating Christmas trees, a tradition that didn't start until the sixteeth century. Instead, it refers to the making of permanent wooden idols. Christmas trees evolved from two Christian symbols.

First, a triangular shelf held Christmas figurines and was topped by a star representing the one that the Magi followed. Second, The Paradise Tree, decorated with apples and white wafers, symbolized the tree of life in the Garden of Eden. Initially, people adorned outdoor trees; then the notion of chopping down trees and moving them indoors followed—first by churches, then the very wealthy, and finally the masses.

The weight of the apples and oranges used for decorations weighed down the branches of all but the largest and sturdiest trees, so German glassblowers began to produce lightweight, glass balls—the first, man-made ornaments—to replace the heavier fruit. Hank Hanegraaff reveals in "Is Christmas Christian?" when Christmas trees were first lighted:

> It is believed that Martin Luther, the Protestant reformer, was the first to light a Christmas tree with candles. While coming home one dark winter's night near Christmas, he was struck with the beauty of the starlight shining through the branches of a small fir tree outside his home. He duplicated the starlight by using candles attached to the branches of his indoor Christmas tree.

By the nineteenth century, Christmas trees were common in Great Britain, and German immigrants brought the tree tradition to America in the 1820s.

VINTAGE POETRY

As shadows cast by cloud and sun
Flit o'er the summer grass,
So, in Thy sight, Almighty One,
Earth's generations pass.

And while the years, an endless host,
Come pressing swiftly on,
The brightest names that earth can boast
Just glisten and are gone.

Yet doth the Star of Bethlehem shed
A luster pure and sweet,
And still it leads, as once it led,
To the Messiah's feet.

And deeply, at this later day,
Our hearts rejoice to see
How children, guided by its ray,
Come to the Saviour's knee.

O Father, may that holy star
Grow every year more bright,
And send its glorious beams afar
To fill the world with light.

THE HOLY STAR
BY WILLIAM CULLEN BRYANT (1794-1878)

STOCKING STUFFER TRADITION
Nativity Treasure Hunt

LESLIE WILSON AND CATHY MESSECAR

Items needed: a nativity set with separate pieces, corresponding scriptures, and clues to direct to hiding places.

Decide where you will hide each piece and make a list. Write out scriptures that correspond with the figurines. Underneath the verse, write a clue to guide children to the figurine. Most of the scriptures may be found in this book under the chapter titles. On the day your family gathers, hide the figurines in your home or even outdoors if weather permits.

Hold back the baby Jesus clue until the end of the hunt. Allow children to discover that the most important person is missing. Then hand them the clue to find baby Jesus with this scripture: "You will find a baby wrapped in cloths and lying in a manger" (Luke 2:12). Hide either the nativity figurine or substitute a more life-like doll wrapped in soft flannel for the children to find.

This activity, enjoyed by adults and children, will help pass along faith and thanksgiving for the baby Jesus—and may be more fun than opening gifts.

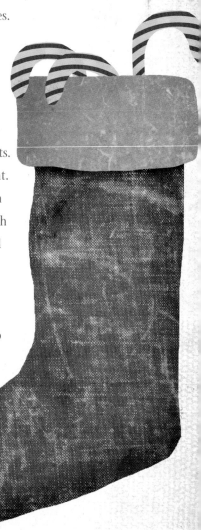

A FEW OF OUR FAVORITE THINGS
Tree Ornaments

BRENDA

Anything handmade by my daughters. Now in their 20s, we have a box of ornaments from their childhood, and it is fun to peek inside each December and go down memory lane.

CATHY

My maternal grandmother and I rarely went shopping together, but one day on such a trip she purchased a partridge tree ornament for me. Grandmother Dora is gone, but the silver bird perches in my tree each year.

KAREN

My mother made beaded frame ornaments. Each holds a photo of my sons when they were young. It's fun to hang them on the tree and show them to their wives and children. Those grands certainly look like their daddies.

LESLIE

My favorite tree ornaments are those my children made throughout the years, especially photos or hand prints. I love to see how they've grown.

TERRA

A glass pickle ornament, a German tradition, that we hide in our tree on Christmas Eve. The first child to see the pickle the next morning is given a small extra gift or, instead of the gift, some families believe the child will have a very fortunate year.

TRISH

The CHRISTmas Nail—a large nail with a ribbon tied to it, hung near the trunk of the tree—symbolic of the nails, the cross, and the sacrifice of Jesus. Purchase one at http://www.christianbook.com/ or make your own by purchasing a large nail at your local hardware store and tying a red ribbon to it.

(T)he word "pageant" is what fifteenth century Englanders called the wagons where mystery plays were performed. Pageant descended from the Latin word *pagina*, which meant platform. By the 1500s, pageant meant a rolling platform, a wagon used as a stage. The wagon and ground in front provided two levels for performances, and extra actors hid underneath the wagon.

Today, pageant refers to a play or event. Some modern pageants are far removed from the simple stable and humble beginnings of The Christ Child. The Tournament of Roses parade in Pasadena, California, is considered a pageant event with floats on wheeled platforms.

PEPPERMINTS FOR LITTLE ONES

Gingerbread Dwellings ~ CATHY MESSECAR

To discover future architects, let children construct mini houses or tents. No blueprints allowed. Give children freedom to use their imaginations.

Ingredients: box of graham crackers, small sealable sandwich bags, small colored candies and other edible foods such as dried fruits. Frosting recipe: 3 egg whites, ½ teaspoon cream of tartar, and 1 pound confectioner's sugar. Mix all and beat 7-10 minutes.

Place a small amount of frosting in a sandwich bag and snip off a bottom corner. Use like a pastry bag to glue walls together. Make sure walls have time to set up, and then allow children to decorate their creations. Walls may be frosted white if desired or candies "glued" straight onto graham crackers.

A GIFT FOR YOU

Cozy Moments ~ The Word Quilters

Homemakers put in overtime during December. The Word Quilters want to say "Thank you" for the loving ways you anchor your family. And remember, be good to yourself. This season follow our suggestions and relax more, stress less.

- Play favorite holiday music in your car and home.
- Drink plenty of water and take vitamins.
- Keep healthy snacks handy.
- Put your feet up. Take a ten-minute break, morning and afternoon.
- At ease—it's okay to trade off a few traditions for a happier more relaxed you.

Let us hear how you do. http://scrapbookofchristmasfirsts.blogspot.com/

COOKIE CANISTER

Big-Big Chocolate Chip Cookies ~ Cathy Messecar

These cookies are large saucer-size, resembling in flavor those sold in shopping malls. Wrap in colored cellophane for gifts. Recipe makes 2 large cookies or it can be doubled to make 4.

⅔ cup shortening or butter ½ tsp. salt

½ cup sugar ½ tsp. soda 1 ½ cups flour

½ cup dark brown sugar 1 6-oz. bag semi-sweet chocolate chips

1 large egg ½ to 1 cup chopped nuts (optional)

Cream shortening, sugars, and egg. Stir in dry ingredients. Add chips and nuts. Divide dough in half. On a lightly oiled cookie sheet or baking stone, pat one portion (½ dough) into 8-inch circle, with ½ -inch thick edges (to avoid crumbling).

Bake at 375° for 12-15 minutes. Completely cool on cookie sheet. Remove with wide spatula.

EVERGREEN THUMB

A Green Christmas ~ TERRA HANGEN

Christmas brings opportunities to make green choices and help the environment: Many communities offer Christmas tree recycling. Trees are chipped, turned into mulch, and used for erosion control in parks, and along rivers and lakes. Sometimes the wood chips are supplied to gardeners.

In some cities, Bass Pro Company collects trees to sink in lakes and reservoirs, which improves fish habitat.

Consider buying strings of LED lights, which use much less electricity than incandescent lights. Washington's National Christmas Tree and the Rockefeller Center Tree now use LED lights for their gorgeous displays.

Buy pretty holiday bags and reuse them year after year, instead of wrapping paper which is thrown away after use. Make gift tags from last year's Christmas cards. Cut the card with pinking shears, hole punch the corner, and attach to gift packaging with ribbon.

Through caretaking of resources, show your appreciation and thanksgiving to the Creator of the Earth.

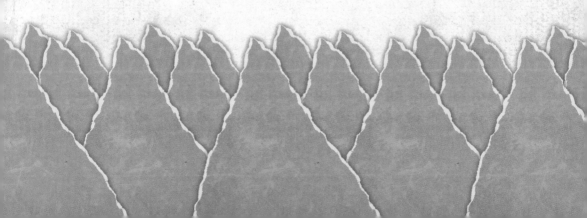

Dad's First Diploma

BY BRENDA NIXON

World War II touched every American. In the opening scenes of that tragedy, my dad, a lanky seventeen-year-old with wavy brown hair and boyish innocence, was a junior at Chillicothe High School nestled in the hills of Southern Ohio. Like his peers during 1943, he walked to school toting schoolbooks and a metal lunchbox, shyly grinned at the girls, dreamed of owning a car someday, and talked about winning the war.

In his small town, patriotic fever spread. Some of the older high school boys began signing their military papers to join after graduation. Although my dad wanted to enlist, he fell below the eighteen-year age requirement.

At home, he shared chores with ten siblings. In their cramped, snug farmhouse, my dad's stepmother hardly spoke to him. Between loads of laundry, meals, and caring for his baby brother, she stayed busy. His father, a stern man with piercing blue eyes, worked all day and left childrearing to his wife. After evening meals, the family gathered around the radio and listened to war news.

Education wasn't a family priority; none of Dad's brothers and sisters received encouragement in academics. And although he anticipated his senior year and graduation, he had no confidence as a student. His feelings of American loyalty and patriotism won out. He decided to quit high school and enlist.

On a hot August morning in 1943, he walked the dusty road to the Army recruiting office.

"How old are ya?" asked the recruiter.

"Eighteen," Dad said, hoping to convince the older man.

"Old 'nuf. Sign here."

With that, seventeen-year-old Robert W. McCorkle enlisted in the military. After basic training at Fort Thomas, Kentucky, he boarded a military ship to Okinawa, Japan, by way of Pearl Harbor just two days after the abrupt attack. At Pearl Harbor, he soberly stared at the still smoky partially submerged battleships.

In rugged Okinawa, Dad operated a loud AAA Machine Gun and served as a Technician Fifth Grade in the Battery Anti-Aircraft Artillery Automatic Weapons Battalion. He shot down enemy planes with precision and witnessed horrors and atrocities that left permanent scars on his memory. By his nineteenth birthday, he was a hardened soldier.

On a crisp March morning in 1946, after his three-year tour of duty, the Army granted Dad an honorable discharge at Camp Atterbury, Indiana, and awarded him the American Theater Ribbon, the Asiatic-Pacific Theater Ribbon with one Bronze Star, a Good Conduct Ribbon, and the Victory Medal. With ribbons proudly displayed on his uniform, Dad returned to his family and tried to fit back into the American way of life.

America welcomed her soldiers home but Dad's return, like many others, grew difficult. Older, saltier, and more mature than other 21-year-olds, he tried to adjust, but his former friends were either married, moved away, wounded in action, or dead. One day he asked his stepmother, "Where's my GI pay?"

"What're you talkin' about?" she asked.

"My military paychecks. I sent them all home these three years."

"You have no money. We needed what you sent, so we spent it. Git yourself a job!"

He felt too ashamed and too old to go back to school and he needed money. Dad found a job as a carpenter, eventually married, and moved into a 12-foot trailer in a mobile home park with other veterans. He continued working as a laborer, building houses. Good at deciphering blueprints, he eventually became job foreman.

Life moved along rapidly for Dad and Mom. With three children, mounting bills and family responsibilities, finishing school became impossible. His youthful days slipped further away and any dream of completing high school faded.

My parents encouraged us to learn. We all went through graduate school and earned master's degrees. As adults, we frequently encouraged Dad to get his GED to fulfill his dream, but something always held him back.

In 2005, I decided my aging father deserved what he'd sacrificed by his decision to serve our country. I contacted the local Veteran Association. "Honorably discharged World War II veterans may receive their actual diploma," the official said. "Just phone his high school and explain." After discreetly gathering documentation and completing all the paperwork, I sent in a request for Dad's diploma.

On Christmas day, our family gathered in the living room encircling my dad. I handed him a thin, square-shaped present.

"What's this?" he asked.

"Just open it," I said.

He carefully pulled away the paper and sat quietly, a bit confused. "High School Diploma," he read aloud.

"You're a graduate, Dad!" I said as tears of pride welled in my eyes. Mom, my sister and brother, and their children applauded.

"You made it!" they all cheered.

Dad's dream didn't die. At 80 years of age, my dad became a high school graduate. Through our gift, we thanked and honored him for his sacrifice.

MORNING STAR LIGHT

Jesus sent him away saying, "Return home
and tell how much God has done for you."
So the man went away and told all over town
how much Jesus had done for him.

LUKE 8:38-39

WORD QUILTERS' WISDOM

Memories of the heart stir gratitude.
Every day say "Thank you."

Brenda Nixon, M.A., former parenting expert for Kansas City's Fox4 Noon News, speaks to issues affecting today's families, helping parents and professionals understand child development and parenting issues. She is the author of *The Birth to Five Book: Confident Childrearing Right from the Start* (Revell/Spring '09), a speaker, media personality, and educator and offers free discipline tips at www.BrendaNixon.com.

Cathy Messecar is a newspaper columnist, author of *The Stained Glass Pickup*, and speaker. She lives on Leaning Tree Acres Farm with her husband, David, in Montgomery, Texas. www.CathyMessecar.com http://stainedglasspickup.blogspot.com/

Karen Robbins, freelance writer and speaker, is also a world traveler, SCUBA diver, mother of five, and the grandmother of six. She writes regularly for www.positivelyfeminine.org and *Lake Erie Living Magazine,* and has contributed to several compilation books. Karen lives with her husband, Bob, in Independence, Ohio. www.KarenRobbins.com

Leslie Wilson pens a weekly humor column, "Reality Motherhood," and makes thousands laugh each year through Hearts at Home, MOPS, and Early Childhood PTAs. She's a contributing author to the *Groovy Chicks' Road Trip series*, *Chicken Soup for the Mother of Preschooler's Soul,* and dozens of parenting magazines. Visit www.RealityMotherhood.com.

Terra Hangen's articles appear in dozens of magazines on subjects including Bible gardening, penguins, flowers and herbs, bicycle soldiers, and prayer. A contributing author to *Rainy Day Book,* and the garden columnist for www.positivelyfeminine.org, she and her husband live in coastal California, where she enjoys gardening while her cats nap in the sun. http://terragarden.blogspot.com/

Trish Berg is a national speaker and author of *Rattled* and *The Great American Supper Swap.* She has been a featured speaker for MOPS International and Hearts at Home, and interviewed on ABC, Focus on the Family, and Midday Connection. Trish lives in Ohio with her husband, Mike, and their four children. www.TrishBerg.com.

Judy Martin Bowyer often writes narratives about her West Texas roots. She and her geriatric cat currently create stories from their home in Petersburg, Texas. www.judymartinbowyer.com

Janet Perez Eckles is a conference speaker, writer, and contributor to ten books, including the *Chicken Soup for the Soul Series* and also to Guidepost books. www.janetperezeckles.com

Charlotte Holt, a freelance writer, speaker, and retired teacher, resides in Kingwood, Texas, with her husband, Charles. Website: www.publishedauthors.net/charlotteholt.

Karen Hood speaks/writes about the power of words. She's led women's Bible studies and writes devotionals and newsletters. kehood@earthlink.net

Linda LaMar Jewel is a writer, speaker, CLASSeminar trainer, and member of Blue Star Mothers, an organization for military moms. www.bluestarmothers.org

Tammy Marcelain is first a wife and mother, and then a wedding photographer (marcelainphotography.com) and Christian speaker (thecoffeegroup.net.) Her greatest love is Jesus.

D'Ann Mateer has written three unpublished novels as well as several published articles and short stories. She blogs regularly at http://fivebazillionandone.blogspot.com

Jeanette Sharp lives in The Woodlands, Texas, with her husband, Jim, and their Shih Tzu, Maggie.

Jan Tickner is a seasoned author, journalist, free-lance writer, and recognized award winner. A widow, this mother of four, grandmother, and great-grandmother resides in a writer-friendly condo in Conroe, Texas.